TWENTY CENTURIES OF ECUMENISM

Commission on Faith and Order
National Council of Churches
475 Riverside Drive   Room 872
New York, N. Y., 10115

Sale

*PAC bought
This book at
a sale!*

TWENTY CENTURIES
OF ECUMENISM

Jacques Elisée Desseaux

Translated by Matthew J. O'Connell

Paulist Press 🕊 *New York/Ramsey*

Library of Congress
Catalog Card Number: 83-62950

ISBN: 0-8091-2617-6

Published by Paulist Press
545 Island Road, Ramsey, N.J. 07446

Printed and bound in the
United States of America

CONTENTS

INTRODUCTION:
FROM BABEL TO PENTECOST

The eleventh chapter of the Book of Genesis tells us that in the beginning "the sons of men" formed a single people and all had but one language (v. 6). But they were already consumed by ambition and were determined to build Babel, that is, Babylon, a city containing "a tower with its top in the heavens" (v. 4), as symbol of a will to power and a lust for worldwide domination.

At this point, Genesis goes on to say, God decides to "confuse their language, that they may not understand one another's speech" (v. 7). The division of languages and everything that follows from this division is thus the consequence of sin. This is the point being made by the Bible as it shows us, in the New Testament, that Jesus Christ establishes a new order of things and a new human race, in which everything is brought into unity in him.

According to our Christian faith Jesus brings the Scriptures to their completion and fulfills the prophecies: "I will gather you from all the nations" (Jer 29:14); "I will gather you out of the countries where you are scattered" (Ez 20:34); "I will gather them from the countries" (Ez 34:12–13). St. John echoes the prophets when he speaks of "one flock, one shepherd" (Jn 10:16).

Paul reminds us that Jesus

> is our peace, who has made us both one, and has broken down the dividing wall of hostility, by abolishing in his flesh

> the law of commandments and ordinances, that he might
> create in himself one new man in place of the two, so mak-
> ing peace, and might reconcile us both to God in one body
> through the cross, thereby bringing the hostility to an end
> (Eph 2:14–17).

As we reread this passage, how can we fail to note in passing
the implications of it for dialogue among Christians and for dialogue between Jews and Christians?

In commenting on Caiaphas' prophecy that "Jesus should
die for the nation," St. John adds: "and not for the nation only,
but to gather into one the children of God who are scattered
abroad" (Jn 11:51–52). The same evangelist records for us in
his seventeenth chapter the prayer which Jesus offered to his
Father: "Keep them in thy name which thou has given me,
that they may be one, even as we are one" (17:11); "Sanctify
them in the truth; thy word is truth. As thou didst send me into
the world, so have I sent them into the world. And for their
sake I consecrate myself, that they also may be consecrated in
truth" (17:17–19).

> I do not pray for these only, but also for those who believe
> in me through their word, that they may all be one; even as
> thou, Father, art in me, and I in thee, that they also may be
> in us, so that the world may believe that thou has sent me.
> The glory which thou hast given me I have given to them,
> that they may be one even as we are one, I in them and
> thou in me, that they may become perfectly one, so that the
> world may know that thou has sent me and has loved them
> even as thou has loved me (17:20–23).

The Acts of the Apostles tell us that on Pentecost the Spirit
worked a miracle of tongues: the apostles "were all filled with
the Holy Spirit and began to speak in other tongues, as the
Spirit gave them utterance. . . . Each one heard them speaking
in his own language" (Acts 2:1-12).

This miracle of tongues reverses the catastrophe of Babel.
Henceforth, human beings can, if they are willing, hear in

their own tongue the common language of the Gospel of Christ.

At Babel, the division of tongues was an outward image of the destruction of human unity by the sin of pride and self-sufficiency.

Pentecost symbolizes the fact that in Christ and by the power of Christ's Spirit the lost unity has been recovered, although in a manner still hidden and lacking its visible manifestation: "We are God's children now," says St. John, but "it does not yet appear what we shall be" (1 Jn 3:2).

We need no reminding of this incompleteness, since everyday reality brings it home to us: we are still subject to heart attacks and cancer, to unemployment and war, to every kind of violence, injustice, misfortune and accident; and we are still laid low by death.

Sin has been vanquished by Christ, but the consequences of sin will not be eliminated until the end of time.

In like manner, unity has been definitively won for us in Christ, but we must constantly accept it and make it a reality for ourselves through self-transcendence and rejection of the sins that divide us and the self-centeredness that sets us against one another: the self-centeredness of individuals, of nations, of cultural ambiances, and of Churches or religious groups.

Unity has been definitively won for us, but the study of history tells us that in a hellish cycle the Church's fabric has until now been rent anew every five centuries. This is the subject of my first chapter: "Past Divisions."

In the sixth century, after the Council of Chalcedon (451), some ancient Churches (in Armenia, Persia, Syria, Egypt and Ethiopia) refused to accept the Council's dogmatic formulation regarding Jesus Christ as true God and true man. For this theological reason, along with others that were not theological, there was a rupture between these Churches, henceforth called "pre-Chalcedonian," and the Churches which remained in union with Constantinople and Rome.

The eleventh century brought the official break between the Western Church and the Orthodox Churches, with reciprocal excommunications being pronounced by Rome and Constantinople.

In the sixteenth century, Luther was excommunicated in 1521. Some Churches joined the Reformation; among others, the English, or Anglican, Church broke with Rome. The Western Church itself was now divided.

These are the chief divisions; every fifth century has brought a new one. And I have said nothing as yet of the divisions which have multiplied within Churches already divided from one another: the schism of the Old Believers in Russia in the seventeenth century; Methodism, a reform which Anglicanism rejected; the "Old Catholic" schism which sprang from opposition to Vatican Council I in the nineteenth century and had been preceded by the schism of Utrecht (1724) in the eighteenth century (the two groups ultimately forming the "Union of Utrecht" in 1899); the fragmentation of the Protestant world into a variety of currents, "denominations" and ecclesiastical organizations.

And now we have the twentieth century: the century of ecumenism.

During the congress of Protestant missionary societies at Edinburgh in 1910 a participant from the Far East addressed the Westerners in words which Pastor Boegner used to love to recall: "You have brought us your divisions. We beg you to preach the Gospel to us and to allow Jesus Christ to raise up through his Spirit a Church set free of all the isms that now influence your preaching of the Gospel among us." The intervention had a decisive effect.

The result was the ecumenical movement. This is the subject of my second chapter: "Reconciliations and Rediscoveries Past and Present." We are now realizing with the help of faith that despite its scandalous and anti-evangelical character the "visible" division among the Churches does not necessarily destroy the unity effected by grace. Unity is more persistent than the divisions, for unity is already given to us and we must constantly accept it.

The gift of unity resides in the Church, in the only Church of Christ. But this only Church is not a single Church; it is not a

Church marked by unity, for when confronted with the requirement of visible unity, all the Churches are found to be unfaithful. This infidelity is a scandal not only to men. (In fact, for men to be scandalized, they must first have become aware of and sensitive to the vocation of the Church.) The scandal exists also, and even essentially, in relation to God. Before the Father and the Lord Jesus and in view of their responsibility to bear witness to the reign of Jesus through the Spirit, the Churches among us are unfaithful. They are a source of scandal because they have wasted the gift of unity in Jesus Christ. The scandal is theological.

On the other hand, it is on the basis of the gift as still given, and despite the infidelity of the Christian communities, that the only Church must regain its unity. Only then will this only Church be the people God wants for himself; only then will the Father be glorified.

The need, then, is for all Christians, all the baptized, to rediscover the meaning of the Church's vocation and lead the Church to conversion so that it may carry out God's will.

In this perspective, ecumenism is not simply a search for communion, as I explain in Chapter III, "Ecumenical Life Today," which deals with the concretizations and forms, the progress and obstacles, the problems and demands of this life. Ecumenism is rather the concerted effort of the Churches, rooted as they are in the one body of Christ, to restore to a communion already existent but weakened the fullness Christ wants it to have. Communion does not need to be established; it does need to find, to rediscover, its complete dimensions.

The ecumenical task is therefore a primordial one, because it is concerned with the fidelity of the Church to its own vocation of bearing witness, through visible unity, to reconciliation and communion.

I.

PAST DIVISIONS

An historian of Christian origins has written that the Church has been in a state of crisis ever since the first Pentecost Monday. His estimate of the situation is quite accurate. For proof we need only glance through the Acts of the Apostles, which sketch the history of the first communities brought into existence by a common faith in Christ, or read the letters which St. Paul wrote to some of them and which are an authentic witness to the life of the first Christians.

St. Paul even dares to say that there must be factions. This postulate, which was also a statement of fact, gave rise to reflection on the spiritual and theological meaning of such divisions. Some saw in them a motive for a greater purity of faith on the part of those who refused to separate themselves from the true Church. Others saw in them also a stimulus to a full and vigilant faith; thus St. Augustine wrote: "If there were no divisions we would find ourselves nodding over the Scriptures."

In the second and third centuries, immediately after the apostolic age (that is, immediately after the days of the apostles), many small heretical groups came into existence. The transitoriness of their existence, together with the limited space available to me here, excuses me from describing them.

Much more serious was the division caused by the heresy

of Arius (beginning in 318). I shall come back to it a bit further on.

In the time of St. Augustine, who died in 430 while his episcopal city Hippo was being besieged by the Arian Vandals, the Donatist schism divided the hitherto flourishing Churches of North Africa.

The violent confrontations of that age were sad foretastes of the attacks made nowadays by some extremists on their "brothers and sisters" in the faith.

There is reason to think that the weakening which Donatism caused and which the invasion of the Arian Vandals aggravated lowered the resistance of African Christianity, so that Islam had little trouble in sweeping Christianity away at the beginning of the eighth century.

Even more serious, however, was another series of events which began in the same period as the Donatist schism and to which I must now turn.

Fifth Century: Separation of the Semitic Churches

Theological Issues

St. John says in his Gospel: "In the beginning was the Word, and the Word was with God, and the Word was God. . . . And the Word became flesh and dwelt among us, full of grace and truth; we have beheld his glory, glory as of the only Son from the Father" (Jn 1:1, 14).

This is the central assertion of the Christian faith. But when the Church, in fidelity to the Gospel, confesses a being who pre-exists in the divine world and has become man, it is faced with two serious problems:

1. What is the relation between God and the Word of God, who is God's Son? This is the problem faced by the theology that in fact developed into a theology of the Trinity, inasmuch as the Christian faith adds the Holy Spirit to the Father and the Son.

2. What is the relation, in the Word made flesh (that is, in Jesus Christ as man and God) between Word and flesh? This is the Christological problem.

The two problems are connected. The first of them is the one that first caught men's attention, and Arianism supplied the occasion for the development of the solution. Arianism, the heretical teaching professed by Arius, a priest of Alexandria, in 318, claimed that the Word is the first of all creatures and not God. The Council of Nicaea responded to this in 325 by defining the faith we profess in the Creed: Jesus Christ is consubstantial with the Father. Such was the first Christian dogma to be formulated. But the Arian heresy was to have millions of adherents, including emperors and bishops, and was to create a division in the Church for a long time.

The second of the two problems was posed in the fifth century. There are two possible approaches to the question of the unity of Christ as true God and true man that was to occupy theologians for three centuries.

The first approach takes for its starting point the beginning of St. John's Gospel where the evangelist contemplates the divine Word dwelling from all eternity in the bosom of the Father and then shows him becoming a human being within time for the salvation of the human race. This is a theology that emphasizes unity. When carried to extremes, it leads to monophysitism, the heresy which swallows up the humanity of Christ in his divinity and was to be professed especially at Alexandria.

The second approach starts from the Synoptic Gospels and with the historical Christ, who is subject to human determinisms (hunger, and so on) which prove him to be human, and who also performs miracles, which prove him to be divine. The next step in the argument is the unity of Christ. This is the dualist or dyophysite theology promoted at Antioch. When carried to extremes, this theology leads to Nestorianism, a heresy which owes its name to Nestorius, patriarch of Constantinople, and which overly separates the humanity and the divinity in

Jesus and says that Mary is mother only of the man Jesus and not Mother of God.

The Council of Ephesus (431) condemned Nestorianism and asserted that Mary can indeed be called Mother of God (Theotokos). The Council of Chalcedon (451) condemned monophysitism at the urging of St. Leo the Great and asserted that Christ is true man and true God in the one divine person (hypostatic union).

In 381 the Council of Constantinople defined the divinity of the Holy Spirit, in order to put an end to the heresy of the Pneumatomachians (deniers of the divinity of the Spirit).

In 553 and 680 the second and third Councils of Constantinople completed the work of Chalcedon by asserting that Christ has two wills, a human and a divine.

Historical Issues

The first major intervention of the political power in the life of the Church was occasioned by Arianism, the first great heresy, when the Emperor Constantine convoked the Council of Nicaea. This did not prevent the spread of Arianism even in official circles and the imperial court.

The development of the disputes over the Spirit and over Christ (Nestorianism, then monophysitism) led to further interventions of the political authorities in the religious sphere, despite the strong protests of the bishops. Like the Council of Nicaea the Councils of Constantinople (381), Ephesus (431) and Chalcedon (451) were all convoked by the emperors.

If we are to grasp all the causes for this first great rending of the Church, namely, the departure so to speak of the Semitic world from the Church, we must situate the various Churches and communities in their historical and political context, since the causes in question were non-theological as well as theological.

At that time the Church in Persia was emerging from a long period of persecution. This Church was located in the vast territory at the far side of what we now call the Middle East. It was an area in which Christianity had experienced a vigorous growth. The population was Syrian and very largely of Semitic extraction. It was descended from the Jews who, according to the Bible, had stayed behind in large numbers when the Babylonian exile came to an end.

The area thus Christianized and thus populated was cut off from Palestine by the Syrian desert but linked to Antioch by Osroene.

It was by this latter corridor that the early disciples had very soon made their way into the territories in which the Church of Persia would subsequently make its appearance. The fact that these early disciples spoke the same language as the peoples there was a major advantage in the effort to introduce Christianity and spread the Gospel.

The Church of Persia cut itself off from the rest of the Church in the fifth century for several reasons:

1. The appeals of the Christians in Persia to the West and especially to Byzantium gave the emperors of Persia a good excuse for launching persecutions. In order to do away with this excuse the bishops in Persia agreed not to appeal to the West in their own doctrinal disagreements.

2. The bishops wanted to be independent of the West and especially of Byzantium lest they appear overly bound to show allegiance in those quarters. Consequently, when Sapor II conquered Julian the Apostate the communities of the Church of Persia were already ripe for a separation which became a reality when in 424 the bishops agreed to bestow on their patriarch, whose see was Ctesiphon, "a primacy like that of St. Peter over the other Churches."

3. The refusal to accept the doctrinal and disciplinary decisions of Ephesus and Chalcedon was a logical consequence and led in turn to a practical schismatic outlook. The Church of Persia declared itself Nestorian and broke off. Independent Churches were then established in Syria and Mesopotamia. They were very missionary in their attitude and spread into Asia as far as China. Of these Churches only small communities remain today, in Iran and in the United States.

The Churches of Egypt (Copts) and Ethiopia likewise rejected the Councils and declared themselves monophysite. There are flourishing monophysite Churches today in Armenia, Georgia, Egypt, Ethiopia, the Levant and the Malabar Coast of India. Echmiadzin is the primatial see of all the Armenians; the Catholicos exercises jurisdiction over the two million Armenians living in the Soviet Union and over most of the emigrés in Europe and America, who number about a million. There are three other jurisdictions in the Middle East: the Catholicate of Cilicia (Lebanon, Syria, Cyprus) and the Patriarchates of Constantinople and Jerusalem (200,000 faithful). A Catholic Armenian patriarchate was established in the sixteenth century and numbers 100,000 faithful.

These divisions had serious consequences, which are brought home to us when we look at the geographical picture. In the Christianity of the early centuries Rome and the West might be said to form the left wing, Byzantium the center, and Persia the right wing. This whole right wing split off. It is worth observing, however, that it did not split off directly from Rome but primarily from the Christendom of imperial Byzantium; it was from this same Christendom of the empire that the Abyssinian and Coptic communities broke off. The absence of the Semitic world from the theological thinking of the other Churches has left a profound mark and shows in a certain imbalance in this thinking, with the scale tipping on the side of Greek thought.

Whatever the role played by non-theological causes of division, it is quite clear that the theological factors which served some communities as occasions or pretexts for leaving the Church were also causes of the separation.

Eleventh Century: Separation of the Church of Rome
and the Church of Constantinople

Estrangement

English-speaking ecumenists use this term to describe the growing rift that culminates in the separation of Christian communities from each other. The break between Rome and

Constantinople is usually dated in 1054, because that was the year in which Cardinal Humbert of Silva Candida (who had been a monk of Moyenmoutier) placed on the altar of Hagia Sophia an excommunication couched in terms that were unacceptable to the Church of Constantinople. Patriarch Michael Cerularius and his Synod met anathema with anathema.

Historians unanimously agree today that in 1054 there was no real schism between the Churches of Rome and Constantinople and that the year 1054 did not become symbolic until the Council of Florence (1430–1439). This Council had for its purpose to re-establish union between East and West and it therefore felt a need to pinpoint the date of separation. As a matter of fact, long before 1054 there had been difficulties which on several occasions led to a break in communion. Ever since the time of Msgr. Duchesne a classic exercise for the historian has been to calculate the number of years of full communion and years of separation. In this connection Fr. Congar says: "One cannot consider 217 years of separation in 506 years of history without realizing that this does not mean normal union simply interrupted by accidents."[1]

On the other hand, well before 1054 there were also facts and actions pointing to canonical communion. The state of separation between the Churches came into existence only very gradually. The break which occurred in 1054 had little influence at first on the many relations between Greeks and Latins, Easterners and Westerners. The dealings with one another might be in the area of business, but they might also concern matters of devotion: Westerners went as pilgrims to Jerusalem, and Easterners betook themselves to Rome, the city where Peter and Paul had confessed the faith. Furthermore, the Byzantine emperors, feeling the threat of the Turks, endeavored to re-establish friendly relations with the Pope and the West. In 1089 the name of Pope Urban II was even reinserted in the diptychs of Constantinople for eighteen months.

The Popes of the second half of the eleventh century believed in all good faith that a Crusade would be a means of bringing East and West together and reuniting them. Gregory VII in his letters and Urban II at Piacenza in 1095 spoke of the expedition to Palestine as essentially a way of helping Byzantium. They hoped that the Crusade would create the conditions needed for the restoration of relations between the Churches. Unfortunately, the result was the direct opposite: the capture of Constantinople in 1204 by the French and Venetians of the Fourth Crusade which had been diverted there proved to be an irreparable disaster that for a long time killed all hopes of reunion.

Innocent III protested strongly against this sidetracking of the Crusade and against the violence and looting that ensued, but he sanctioned the fait accompli by appointing a Latin patriarch and installing Latin bishops in many Greek sees.

The event of 1054 was to be a point of crystallization for all the forces working against unity and all the causes of separation, to which I now turn.

The Separation and Its Causes

Seventy years after the siege of Constantinople by the Crusaders the Council of Lyons was held (1274), which has come to be known, since Paul VI, as "the sixth of the general synods held in the West."[2] In the intention of Pope Gregory X, who convoked it, this Council was to bring about a restoration of unity, but the goal was not achieved. In 1439 the Council of Florence likewise ended in failure. The reunions decreed at Lyons and Florence were equally shaky, partly because they were up against dynamisms which favored separation, and partly because they were proclaimed "at the top" without any participation by the people at the base of the pyramid and were therefore not accepted by the latter. Reception in the course of time is, after all, a process essential to faith and life of the Church.

I cannot treat the subject exhaustively, nor shall I attempt to do so, but let me at least say briefly what the causes of this separation were. They were to some extent theological but they were first and foremost non-theological.

In the political sphere, first of all, the situation had become increasingly different in East and West ever since the barbarian invasions. The establishment of the Holy Roman

Empire of the West by the crowning of Charlemagne in 800 had shocked the East. The crowning of Otto I in 962 and his seizure of power over Rome meant to Easterners that Otto was seeking a universal hegemony, and they began to regard the Popes with increasing distrust. The latter had backed the creation of the Western empire and was often appointed by its ruler. When the Pope thus separated himself from the unity of the ancient Roman-Byzantine empire, was he not also separating himself from the unity of the Church?

In the cultural sphere the barbarized West was regarded with some contempt by the East with its heritage of secular and religious culture; the West therefore tried to free itself from this cultural colonization by creating a culture of its own. Even external practices or customs became grounds for disagreement and opposition—for example, that priests were bearded in the East but clean-shaven in the West, and that unleavened bread was used for the Eucharist in the West but leavened in the East. Divergent mentalities hardened, and the result was distrust, suspicion and mutual condemnation.

At the theological level, with the acculturation to be found there on each side, we can see differences of perception, sensibility and expression. The East is very contemplative. It goes straight to the mystery of the invisible, that is, of the revelation of the Glory through the visible. It contemplates the mystery of God as seen in the revelation of the Son and in the human-divine mystery of the Church. It was the East that developed Trinitarian theology and Christology.

The West, on the other hand, is more pragmatic in its outlook, and its theology has been concerned rather with questions of salvation and the means of salvation, with problems of ecclesiology and the sacramental life. What is the Church? What is grace?

Again at the theological level, the ministry proper to the bishop of Rome became a point of friction and division. At the time of the Councils of Ephesus and Chalcedon East and West already had different conceptions of the relation between Pope and Council.[3] Nor did they share the same vision of the part to be played by the Church of Rome and its bishop in the service of universal communion. In the view of the East, the local Church of Rome, with its bishop, was to preside over the union of the Churches in love. The West, on the other hand, was increasingly bent on attaching to this presidency a jurisdiction and even a hegemony over the other Churches. The West reached the point of "attributing to the bishop of Rome a personal authority which was regarded as unqualified in terms of the obedience it called for, as unlimited in its object, and, should occasion arise, as arbitrary in its exercise" (Msgr. Dumont). The tradition regarding the papacy was considered by the West to originate in the apostles; it was "apostolic." In the East it was regarded simply as a matter of ecclesiastical law. The expression "the Church of Rome, Mother and Mistress," which became increasingly predominant in the West, to the detriment of the idea of "Sister Churches," suggested a theology of unqualified domination.

This, then, was a serious theological bone of contention. There was another: the *Filioque.* In 431, the Council of Ephesus had decreed that there were to be no additions made to the conciliar creeds. However, the Latin theologians of Charlemagne, in order to counter the Adoptianism which was sweeping Spain at that time, managed to impose on the Western Church the formula: "The Holy Spirit proceeds from the Father and the Son," whereas the Council of Constantinople (381) had said simply: "The Holy Spirit proceeds from the Father."

The question of purgatory and the dogmas of the Immaculate Conception and Assumption were later added to the original points of theological disagreement. In addition, the Orthodox reproached the West (not without some justification) for neglecting the invocation of the Holy Spirit (the epiclesis) and for downplaying the important role of the Holy Spirit in the sacramental, theological, liturgical and practical life of the Church.

On the whole, then, the separation between Rome and Constantinople was a break between hierarchies, which eventually made it canonically impossible for these hierarchies and for the faithful on the two sides to celebrate the liturgy together and to share the Eucharist.

Two final remarks are in order. For the first I may quote the words of Vatican II's *Decree on Ecumenism:* "In the study of revealed truth East and West have used different methods and approaches in understanding and confessing divine things" (no. 17).[4] But in an atmosphere favorable to a break in relations diversity turned into separation.

The second remark—one often made by theologians and historians—is that once this separation removed the counterbalancing fraternal and contemplative influence exerted by the sister Church of Constantinople, the Church of Rome was unable to safeguard itself against the excesses of its own tendencies. The separation of the eleventh century carried within it, in germinal form, the causes of the defects that led to the tragedy of the sixteenth century.

Sixteenth Century: Breakdown of the Western Church

A Very Complex Matter

The divisions which took place in the West were quite complicated. In some countries (the Scandinavian, for example), whole communions joined the Reformation. In others, however, as in France, the division cut across one and the same people and communion. In addition, some of these communions preserved Catholic traditions and structures, at least in practice if not in theory; I am thinking here of the Lutheran Church and especially of the Anglican Church which claims to be in continuity with the historical episcopate, reads the Bible according to the tradition of the Fathers, and carries on a liturgical and dogmatic life that is inspired by the ecumenical Councils of the undivided Church of the first four centuries.

There is thus a complex diversity to be found in the communions that have sprung from the work of the Reformers, from the various baptist or revivalist religious movements, and from movements of separation from Rome.

Reform "In Head and Members"

In his book *One and Holy* Karl Adam writes: "Modern historians are agreed that the roots of the Reformation reach far back into the high Middle Ages."[5]

As far back as the twelfth century, we find Gerhoh of Reichersberg (1093–1169), a German who had remained loyal to the papacy during the Investiture Controversy and had even suffered exile on this account, expressing concern over the dangers threatening the Church; in his final work, *The Fourth Watch of the Night,* he sees the end of his age coming in the form of corruption that is inspired by avarice and is turning Rome into a second Babylon. His words remind us of the warning which St. Bernard, a contemporary of Gerhoh, addresses to his former disciple, Pope Eugene III, in his *De consideratione:* "Pay heed! You are becoming the Church of Constantine and not of Peter. When you don your purple cloak and ride your white horse, you act like the Church of Constantine. Where do you get such notions? Not from Peter but from Constantine."

In the thirteenth century, William Durandus, bishop of Mende, writes in his *De modo generalis concilii celebrandi* (a report preparatory for the Council of Vienne in 1311): "If the urgently needed reform of the Church's head and members is not carried out, things will get increasingly worse and the entire evil will be laid at the door of the Holy Father, the cardinals and the Council."

During that same century St. Catherine of Siena writes to Pierre d'Estaing, papal legate for Italy: "You must work with the Holy Father and make every effort to ward off from the sheepfold those wolves, those incarnate demons who think only of good living and splendid palaces and fine carriages and horses. Alas, what Christ won on the wood of the cross is spent on kept women."

Confessions

Well into the fifteenth century, Cardinal Giuliano Cesarini, whose letter Bossuet prints at the beginning of his *Histoire des variations,* wrote as follows to Pope Eugene IV (1431–47):

All these disorders stir popular hatred against the entire ecclesiastical order, and if they are left uncorrected, it is to be
feared that the laity will hurl themselves upon the clergy,
after the fashion of the Hussites, as they openly threaten to
do. The Bohemian heresy will be followed by another even
more dangerous, for it will be said that the clergy are incor-
rigible and cannot bear to have their disorders set right.
People will attack us once they have no longer any hope of
our being corrected. The minds of men wait expectantly for
what we will do, and it seems that they will soon take some
tragic step. They will soon come to believe that they are offering a pleasing sacrifice to God by mistreating or despoil-
ing ecclesiastics, on the ground the latter are hateful to God
and men and have plumbed the depths of evil. The little devotion to the sacred order that is left will be lost. All the disorders of the clergy will be blamed on the court of Rome,
which will be regarded as the source of all evils. I see the
axe set to the root and the tree bending; instead of support-
ing it while there is still time, we are hurling it to the
ground.

On the very eve of the Reformation Cardinal Aleander
wrote to Pope Leo X: "For the love of God, I and all Catholics
with me ask that an end be put to all these reservations, dis-
pensations, provisions and expectations that are connected
with benefices. No one here in Germany has any desire to reject God, but they do want vengeance on these enormous
abuses."

At almost that very moment the Holy See was granting a
Hohenzollern, Albert of Brandenburg, a license to preach in-
dulgences, in exchange for a dispensation allowing an accumu-
lation of benefices (although such accumulations had been
condemned by all the Councils for several centuries now). This
preaching, organized at Wittenberg and so clumsily managed
by the Dominican Tetzel, was to be the occasion for Luther's
"protest."

With the papal legate Chieregati acting as his representative, the last Germanic Pope, Adrian VI, made the following
public confession at the Diet of Nuremberg on January 3,

1523: "We frankly acknowledge that God permits this persecution of his Church on account of the sins of men, and especially of prelates and clergy. . . . We know well that for many years things deserving of abhorrence have gathered round the Holy See; sacred things have been misused, ordinances transgressed, so that in everything there has been a change for the worse. . . . We shall use all diligence to reform before all things the Roman Curia whence, perhaps, all these evils have had their origin."[6]

At the second session of the Council of Trent (which had begun in 1545 when Luther had only a few months to live), Cardinal Reginald Pole, well known for his admirable efforts to restore Catholicism in England, addressed the fathers of the council in his capacity as papal legate:

> We shepherds must hold ourselves responsible before the tribunal of divine mercy for all the evils now afflicting the flock of Christ. For clearly it is our ambitiousness, our avarice, our greed that have brought these evils upon the people of God, and it is because of these sins that pastors are expelled from their Churches, the Churches are deprived of the word of God, the material goods of the Church, which belong to the poor, are looted, and the priesthood is conferred upon unworthy men who differ from the laity only by their garments. If God had punished us as we deserve, we would long since have been treated like Sodom and Gomorrah.

In his General Introduction to the first volume of the *Nouvelle Histoire de l'Eglise* Roger Aubert observes that "these confessions, so impressive in their brutal candidness, are simply the application of a sound theology of the Church,"[7] the very theology in fact which Vatican II has taught us and which John XXIII, Paul VI and John Paul II have begun to apply in their desire that there be mutual forgiveness of wrongs done.

In summary, it is clear to us as we look back that the Church lived for three centuries in a situation which no one tried seriously to remedy. It was a situation marked by abuses and deviations in three areas: pastoral government (simony, manner of rule, immorality), piety (exaggerated devotions and superstitions), and theology (decadent Scholasticism and nominalism in which Luther, Calvin and so many others were formed and whose influence and role we must neither minimize nor exaggerate).

Great Schism, Renaissance and German Nationalism

Not the least of all the evils was the scandal given to the whole of Christendom by the great Western schism, that major internal conflict in the Roman Church which at the end of the fourteenth century and the beginning of the fifteenth saw two and, soon thereafter, three Popes laying claim to the episcopal see of Rome.

Meanwhile a far-reaching evolution was taking place in the world at large as the Middle Ages came to an end and the modern age dawned. This was the age of the Renaissance. The very word expresses the profound change that was occurring in manners and mentalities, that is, in the ways in which men and women thought, felt, expressed themselves, behaved, and established frames of reference. The change found its voice in the artistic and aesthetic sphere and in philosophy where a new way of understanding man and making him his own center was gradually established.

Scientific and geographic discoveries hastened the process even more. Though turned to the future, the Renaissance was at the same time influenced by the rediscovered heritage of classical and pagan antiquity. Naturalism, moreover, was reinforcing the new anthropocentrism.

Nor must we leave out of account the pressures of the nationalisms that were causing a breakup of the West, which until now had been more or less united by the ideal of a single Christendom as a supranational group of peoples whom a single faith united around the papacy as a common center.

From this point of view many historians see Luther as the man who provided a focus for German nationalism. Treitschke, for example, says of him: "Luther set Germany free and inspired the state, society, the family and science. He gave a flesh and blood embodiment to the inner being of the nation. He was blood of our blood, the German man par excellence."

In an epitaph which he composed for himself Luther wrote that God had sent him to the Germans. His *Address to the Christian Nobility of the German Nation* is filled with nationalistic rhetoric that anticipates Fichte's fourteen *Addresses to the German Nation* (winter of 1807–1808).

We are all familiar with the final stanza of a famous hymn by Luther: "If they take our life, / Wealth, name, child and wife— / Let everything go: / They have no profit so; / The kingdom ours remaineth."[8] We know, too, of the valuable but also embarrassing support that the "Reformation" movement received from the German princes.

In summary, I think Friedrich Heer's judgment is rather accurate: "Protestantism is the child of the Catholicism of the final medieval period."

Let me warn the reader: the superficial description I have given of the state of Christendom at the end of the Middle Ages, and my recall of ecclesiastical admissions regarding many persistent abuses, are not meant to make us view the Reformation as simply a denunciation of the existing situation. Only because this situation was indicative of a loss of spiritual and pastoral meaning did the Reformers—both those who maintained their allegiance to the Catholic Church no matter what the cost, and those who wanted the Church to be different and therefore ended up with a new Church—undertake their work of reform.

Spiritual and Pastoral Motives

In his *Vraie et fausse réforme dans l'Eglise* Yves Congar expressed himself in these strong terms:

> Luther and his rivals were largely inspired by pastoral motives when they undertook the work of reform; they acted in the name of the needs of souls. The idea of freeing men's consciences and of giving them peace, consolation, trust in Jesus Christ and assurance of their salvation recurs often in

Luther and also in Calvin . . . who stated clearly that moral
defects were not a sufficient reason for establishing a new
Church. . . . Both men denounced pastoral abuses . . . and at-
tacked in particular the disastrous state of preaching. . . . It
is impossible to read unmoved Luther's harsh denunciation:
"Would that my adversaries felt the deep pain I feel when I
hear things never written or defined being preached in the
Church of Christ."[9]

In 1517 Luther wanted to initiate a public debate, for despite all his efforts he was unsuccessful in bringing others to
recognize the correctness of many of his intentions. It was at
this point that he thought he could discern a deep and radical
discrepancy between Roman authority and the Gospel. Caught
between, on the one side, the freedom which the Gospel offers
and which he had authenticated by his own religious experience and, on the other, the Church, he saw no solution but to
reject the authority of the Pope.

The problem, as the Reformers saw it, was this: "Can we
be silent about our convictions which are based on Scripture?
Since the Church refuses to obey what we consider to be the
certain truth of the word of God, must we not leave the
Church?" When the alternatives were put in this way, the
choice was inevitable. The key responsibilities which these
men took on themselves dated from the time before they accepted an option couched in such terms.

The year 1517 saw the conclusion in Rome of the Fifth
Lateran Council which had claimed to be a reform Council but
which, according to Luther, "had concerned itself solely with
clothing and shoes" before issuing a call for a further Council,
which would in fact begin only in 1545, a few months before
the death of the Reformer.

Let me try to sum up the spiritual and ecclesiological intu-
itions of nascent Protestantism. One thing is quite clear: Luther moved from a religion of works to a Christianity of pure
faith. A man deeply anxious about his own salvation, he had
discovered with astonishment that man cannot buy God's forgiveness by works or penances and that instead he is justified

by grace which comes through faith in Christ. Luther sought
to free the Church from the morass in which it found itself and
to cleanse it by a return to its sources: first the Scriptures, then
the Fathers. Historical study has shown us that the expansion
of Protestantism is to be explained by the fact that many Christians shared Luther's desires. Unfortunately, the atmosphere
of the time was one that, on both sides, promoted a break; on
the side of the Reformers and on the Catholic side there was
an increasing rigidity to the point where separation became inevitable.

The difference in the approach to the mystery of salvation
and in the way of expressing it, especially as regards relations
between man and God, likewise hardened into an irreducible
opposition.

The Reformers, heavily influenced by the Augustinian tradition, had so strong a sense of God's transcendence and man's
sinfulness that for them the human person is as it were constantly crushed by his sins and never really justified or changed
interiorly. Even when he lives in Christ the Savior, man remains incapable of "cooperating in his own salvation." God
does everything. This radicalism explains the later Protestant
antipathy to Mary who is always suspected of being, if not a
substitute for, at least too closely associated with the all-power-
ful grace of God. Luther himself, however, wrote a magnifi-
cent commentary on the *Magnificat.*

In the sphere of ecclesiology, where they were likewise
under the influence of Augustinianism, the Reformers exaggerated the distinction between the visible Church and the invisible Church to the point of suspecting and even rejecting
everything that is institutional, visible, ritual and sacramental,
everything they feared might serve as a fetter on the sovereign and transcendent freedom of God. This, it is clear, was the
perspective they adopted in the dispute over ministry.
Churches of the Catholic type maintain that Christ's mediation
is rendered present and visible through his ministers; in their
view, the apostolic ministry gives structure to the Church. For
Luther, on the other hand, the only important thing at the

structural level is the common priesthood of the baptized. Calvin's outlook, however, is closer to the faith of the Churches of the Catholic type.

It may be said that certain modern disagreements in matters of ethics and morality can be explained by those original divergences. The latter are in process of being considerably reduced today, as we shall see when we discuss the tendency toward communion that marks contemporary dialogue.

Unfortunately, in a quite understandable reaction to the Protestant Reformation, the Catholic side developed a "Counter-Reformation" theology. This theology was incapable of seeing the properly Catholic elements that were at the basis of Protestantism. It seemed, in addition, to reduce Catholic doctrine to a matter of pure and simple opposition to the Protestant Reformation, and to regard membership in the Church of Christ as based on the acceptance of the Pope's authority.

Meaning of the Word "Protestant"

On April 19, 1529, in reaction against the decree of the Diet of Speyer that forbade any propagation of the new religious ideas, five princes and sixteen cities of the Empire proclaimed (Latin: *protestantes:* declaring publicly, bearing witness, protesting) certain demands made on them by their consciences: "In matters concerning the glory of God and the salvation and blessedness of human beings, each individual must appear before God and render an account of himself. . . . We bear witness (*protestamur*) that we cannot consent to any act or decree that is contrary to God, his holy word and the salvation of men."

Anglicanism: An Historical Accident

As serious historians like the Anglican Carpenter and the Catholic Hughes have said, the English Reformation was a kind of historical accident. Its subsequent developments were more serious than the initial break, which was far from being irremediable.

It is clear that while the break in communion between the

Church of England and Rome was accepted by almost all the English Catholics of the time, it was motivated primarily by reasons that were not doctrinal or religious.

As Geneviève Colas explains in an excellent pamphlet, *Notes sur la Communion Anglicane* (Centre Unité Chrétienne), the Church of England already had its own tradition, which was connected with the English temperament. It preserved this tradition while introducing into it "Protestant" ideas which were regarded as a source of purification for what could be retained of that tradition, and not as a source of elimination. The Anglican Church has always remained faithful to this line of thought. Its determination and certainty of being one and the same Church before and after the Reformation have been clearly expressed by Bishop Bell: "Let us strongly insist that the Church that underwent this reform is the Church that already existed before the Reformation and has continued to be the same Church, although in a reformed state."

Henry VIII did not intend to establish a new Church but to reform the old one. When he removed English Christians from the jurisdiction of the Pope by declaring himself "Supreme Head of the Church of England" after his divorce in 1533, his intention was simply to reassert an ancient tradition of the Catholic Church in England, but one that had been increasingly played down for two centuries. In the sixth century, when the Church of England (*Ecclesia Anglicana*) had been fully established under the authority of St. Augustine of Canterbury, whom Pope Gregory the Great had sent in 596, English Christians had a tradition of ecclesiastical autonomy which was required by the English spirit of independence but was also compatible with the acknowledgement of papal primacy. In the medieval period, however, conflicts arose between the papacy and the monarchy; in the fourteenth and fifteenth centuries the abuses of Rome, the increasing desire of the English Catholics for freedom, and the early Protestant ideas that were abroad (they were reading Luther at Cambridge as early as 1523) prepared the way for the secession of which Henry VIII's divorce was only the occasion.

In 1531 the king's wife, Catherine of Aragon, was getting on in years and was now barren as well; the king therefore conceived the idea of marrying Ann Boleyn. He asked Pope Clement VII to authorize the English bishops to pronounce his first marriage null. In 1534, angered at not having gotten what he wanted, he severed all ties between the Church in his kingdom and the Holy See which had continued to procrastinate. He emancipated the Church from papal jurisdiction, but at the same time he was firmly determined to maintain the Catholic faith among his subjects. He proved this by the law of the Six Articles ("the whip with six strings," as the Protestants called it).

Before this entire lamentable affair Henry VIII had received from the Pope the title of "Defender of the Christian Faith" because he had written a treatise against the ideas of the Reformers. He continued to show his desire of remaining in the great Catholic tradition, as is clear from this letter which Tunstall wrote to Pole at the king's order: "You imagine that the king has turned away from the unity of Christ's Church and wants to separate his Church of England from communion with the body of Christendom. You are wrong. His plan and full intention are in no way to separate himself from the unity of the Catholic Church of Christ but rather to preserve this unity and keep it always intact."

Unlike the various continental Reformations, the Reformation in England originated not in the dogmatic thinking of a Reformer but in the religious politics of a prince, which were in turn determined by his personal situation. The Reformation would in any case undoubtedly have affected England; in point of fact, it made its way into England as a result of the divorce of Henry VIII. The divorce may not have been the cause, but it certainly set everything in motion.

In 1547 Edward VI, son of Henry VIII and Jane Seymour, ascended the throne of England. He was only nine years old, and his protectors, first Somerset and then Warwick, really governed the country. It was they who drew England into the Reformation.

Thomas Cranmer, archbishop of Canterbury and a man already "won over to the new knowledge," gave them zealous aid. He composed the Book of Common Prayer and then the Ordinal. In 1552 he won acceptance of the Forty-Two Articles of religion, which were Calvinist in their inspiration.

Under Mary Tudor (daughter of Catherine and Henry VIII) there was a clumsily handled and temporary return of Catholicism. The political genius and uncompromising firmness of Elizabeth I (daughter of Ann Boleyn and Henry VIII) would achieve more or less of a balance between Catholic and Reformed tendencies.

From this reign on, the sovereign no longer had the title "Supreme Head of the Church" but simply that of "Supreme Governor in All Cases Ecclesiastical and Civil." We must note in this context that the Church of England is by no means subject to the king and Parliament. Only the two ecclesiastical chambers are empowered to formulate laws for the Church; these laws must then receive the approval of the king and Parliament, who thus have the power to "embarrass" the Church, but, as has been said, "to 'embarrass' the Church is not to 'run' the Church."

Elizabeth I promulgated the "Thirty-Nine Articles of Religion" which in tenor and formulation are broad and flexible enough to be interpreted in either a Catholic or a Protestant sense. In 1967 the archbishops of York and Canterbury appointed a commission to revise the Thirty-Nine Articles. These articles bear witness to the "comprehensiveness" so dear to the English genius and so alien to continental minds. Comprehensiveness "is based not on a vague tolerance but on the conviction that conflicts and tensions give rise to truth, and on the belief that this same truth will serve as a balance to the freedom allowed the individual."

In his memorable book, *Nations Have Souls,* André Siegfried has clearly shown how this comprehensiveness is inherent in British empiricism.

Alan Richardson, Anglican canon of Durham, once defined as follows this "glorious comprehensiveness": "A determination to grant others, within the widest possible reasonable limits, the same freedom of views that one claims for oneself."

This typically British and Anglican principle has made it possible for the Anglican Church to look upon itself as a synthesis of Catholic and Evangelical values.

Let me get back to the history of the break in communion. In this regard one fact is rather striking: the minimal resistance Henry VIII encountered when he declared himself "Supreme Head of the Church of England." Only a few Franciscans, Augustinians and Carthusians, a bishop, John Fisher, and a layman, Thomas More, resisted, the last two being decapitated in 1535.

Elizabeth I died in 1603. At that point Anglicanism had already acquired the essential features by which we recognize it today. On the other hand, it asserted itself formally as such only in 1662, the year when the fifth Book of Common Prayer was promulgated and when for practical purposes the Reformation period was over. At the end of the sixteenth century some communities abandoned the Anglican Church which they accused of being excessively subservient to the state by reason of its "establishment." These communities called themselves Congregational Churches and emphasized the autonomy of the local parish. Members of these Churches were among the first emigrants to the United States, the "Pilgrim fathers."

The beginning of the seventeenth century saw the establishment of the Baptist Church. This comprised the Anabaptists and Mennonites who had made their appearance in the sixteenth century and were opposed to infant baptism on the grounds that a personal conversion and profession of faith must precede baptism (the latter being, in addition, by immersion only).

OTHER DIVISIONS IN THE EIGHTEENTH CENTURY AND LATER

In 1666 the Russian Orthodox Church experienced a schism when a sizable minority rejected various liturgical and canonical reforms. This schism (*raskol*) of the Old Believers

(*Starovery*) won a good many new adherents when on January 25, 1721 Tsar Peter the Great, after having suppressed the Patriarchate of Moscow (which the Patriarchate of Constantinople had recognized in 1589), replaced it with the Holy Synod and forced the Church to accept far-reaching reforms. The Old Believers themselves later split into two communities, the Popovtsy and the Bezpopovtsy, the latter of which denied the need of any priesthood.

In 1713 the Roman Catholic Church likewise suffered a schism when the archbishop of Utrecht refused to accept the Bull *Unigenitus* which condemned Jansenism. Some Dutch Catholics followed him in his opposition. In the nineteenth century this group was augmented by those German and Swiss Catholics who followed Ignaz von Döllinger (1799–1890) in rejecting the definition of papal infallibility in 1870. The entire group is known as the "Old Catholics"; its communities are located chiefly in Germany, the Netherlands and Poland.

Around 1750 the Anglican Church was afflicted by a new division within itself, when John Wesley founded the Methodist Church. Wesley was very much influenced by Count N. L. von Zinzendorf, a German Lutheran who at Herrnhut in Saxony had reorganized the Moravian Brethren, disciples of John Huss.

In the Philippines at the beginning of the twentieth century, the Philippine Independent Church, also known as the Aglipayans, broke off from the Roman Catholic Church.

A Polish National Church, made up of Polish Catholics who had emigrated to the United States, was established in 1904.

In these pages I have been describing, with as much objectivity as possible, the actual facts of divisions and separations. It is impossible, however, not to sense the violence and hatred, the tortures and deaths, that accompanied these dramatic shifts of allegiance.

I am reminded here of Voltaire's pessimistic comment: "The shameful disputes among Christians have used religion to cause more confusion and shed more blood than all the political conflicts which devastated France and Germany under pretext of maintaining the balance of Europe." Closer to our own day, Hans Urs von Balthasar exclaimed at the Semaine des Intellectuels Catholiques de France in November 1963:

> This is not what Christ meant or was trying to bring about! Not the Peace of Constantine, not the Carolingian Empire, not the Crusades, still less the Albigensian War, and still less again a Christendom torn into two, three, ten, a hundred shreds! Not the erudite, rigid textbook theologies ranged in battle against one another, nor the clericalism, nor the missionary methods that have been applied for so long now that the damage seems irremediable! Think of all the waste, all the blunders, all the time lost![10]

II.

RECONCILIATIONS AND
REDISCOVERIES
PAST AND PRESENT

DATES, EVENTS, PERSONS

As we have just been seeing, every five centuries there has been a new break in unity. In keeping with this kind of hellish and satanic process ("Satan" means "divider," does it not?), should not the twentieth century likewise be a time of separation? Very much the contrary, for today the spirit of unity and communion is more strongly at work than the spirit of division. Ours is the century of the ecumenical movement, of ecumenism. But why ecumenism?

In order to answer this question I must go back to the idea of theological and non-theological factors which, as we saw, played a part in explaining how past separations came about.

Among the non-theological factors at work in ecumenism there is, first of all, the desire to rise above particularisms in a world tormented by the need for universalism. The growing solidarity of human beings is characterized by interaction and interdependence at the world level. Human beings are increasingly seeing themselves as jointly responsible members of a single human family. We are experiencing the gradual rise of a world consciousness. Now, for those Christians who are most alert and responsive (those who make an effort to discern "the signs of the times"), there is a profound correlation between this unification of the human race and the universality of Christian salvation. These Christians are intensely aware that the Church's mission is to be the witness, the presence, and the place of salvation for every human being. They are convinced, too, that in a world which is undergoingffunification only a Church which is *one* can carry out in a fully adequate way the Christian mission of proclaiming the Gospel. It has therefore become increasingly difficult for these men and women to accept the division of the Churches. Everything that still prevents Christians from living and acting in full communion is a source of suffering for them.

Another factor is the challenge which various forms of atheism issue to the Christian faith: the aggressive ideological atheism of Marxism, the atheism of a materialistic society. There is a growing awareness of the spiritual, moral, intellectual and material afflictions under which the human beings of our time labor. All this imposes on all Christians the obligation of a common service and a common witness and thereby compels them to become newly conscious of the scandal of their divisions. Above all, it rouses a determination to join forces in serving Christ in their unfortunate, oppressed and suffering brothers and sisters and in celebrating together "the sacrament of the poor."

In a world characterized by all sorts of violence, insecurity and outrage Christians join all men and women of good will in coming to the same conclusion as Albert Camus: "The world needs real dialogue . . . falsehood is just as much the opposite of dialogue as *silence,* and . . . the only possible dialogue is between people who remain what they are and speak the truth."[1]

Such, then, in very brief summary, are the non-theological factors at work in the reconciliations and rediscoveries; these factors have exerted their influence especially in our twentieth century because the Holy Spirit has set in motion a dynamic thrust toward communion. There is no denying, however, that theological factors have played an even more determining role, as under the action of the Spirit Christians have become at once more attentive and more responsive to the word of

God, to prayer, and to the unity which was the mission of Christ who died "to gather into one the children of God who are scattered abroad" (Jn 11:52).

As early as 1890, Father Portal and Lord Halifax instituted the method proper to ecumenical conversations when the two men prayed and meditated together on John 17, there above the *caminho novo*, the new road leading from Funchal to the sea. In like manner, all Christians who travel this new road are (in the words of Father Portal himself) being led back to the center, that is, to Christ who is Way, Truth, Life, Reconciliation and Unity. They are determined that through him alone they will together receive, in the Spirit, the Church which comes from the Father.

Let me turn now to a study of the reconciliations and rediscoveries past and present, as history has moved from centuries of separation to the century of ecumenism, and from a dynamic focused on division and causing the failure of every attempt at reunion, to a dynamic focused on communion and leading, despite all opposition, to reconciliation and reunion in the Spirit.

Reconciliations and Rediscoveries between East and West

Dialogues between the pre-Chalcedonian Churches and the Church of Rome have led to some joint declarations.

In October 1971 Paul VI and the Syrian patriarch, Mar Ignatius Jacob III, proclaimed their "agreement that there is no difference in the faith they profess concerning the mystery of the Word of God made flesh and become really man, even if over the centuries difficulties have arisen out of the different theological expressions by which this faith was expressed."[2] In May 1973 Paul VI and the Coptic patriarch of Alexandria, Amba Shenouda III, issued a joint declaration to the same effect.[3]

As far as relations between the Church of Constantinople and the Church of Rome were concerned, the break of 1054 initially had little effect on the many contacts between Greeks and Latins in matters whether of business or of devotion.

Down through the centuries partial reunifications were achieved between local Eastern Churches and the Church of Rome, but the effect was to undermine the unity of the Orthodox Church. The end result was quite different from what the Council of Florence was seeking, namely, an all-inclusive union. I am referring to a phenomenon bearing a name which ought to be avoided: "uniatism." The existence of the Uniate Churches eventually led to the establishment of a Roman Congregation in charge of the Easterners in union with Rome—for example, the "Coptic Catholics," the "Syrian Catholics," the Maronites, and so on. The Congregation adopted the name of "Congregation for the Oriental Churches." The Second Vatican Council passed the *Decree on the Eastern Catholic Churches* that was in fact one of its most bitterly contested documents, less because of its content than because of its opportuneness; the Decree legislates only for Eastern Catholics in their relations with the Orthodox.

The question is often asked: What do the Easterners united to Rome represent in terms of Christian unity? In other words: What role does uniatism play in ecumenism? There are several overlapping answers: that of the secular onlooker who doubtless thinks that uniatism is the pledge and anticipation of the desired full reunion; that of the specialist in these matters who believes that, on the one hand, the limited extent of uniatism makes it a formidable obstacle to unity but that, on the other, it has made the Roman Church aware of the inalienable rights of those Easterners not united to Rome, as the Second Vatican Council has shown. There is also the answer of the Easterners not united to Rome, who think that willingness to discuss this problem is an act of good will on the part of the Roman Church. Finally, there is the point of view of the Uniates themselves as formulated by Melkite Catholic Patriarch Maximos IV in a lecture given at Düsseldorf in August 1960:

We have, therefore, a twofold mission to accomplish within the Catholic Church. We must fight to ensure that Latinism and Catholicism are not synonymous, that Catholicism remains open to every culture, every spirit, and every form of organization compatible with the unity of faith and of love. At the same time, by our example, we must enable the Orthodox Church to recognize that a union with the great Church of the West, with the See of Peter, can be achieved without their being compelled to give up Orthodoxy or any of the spiritual treasures of the apostolic and patristic East which is open toward the future no less than toward the past.

If we remain faithful to this mission, we shall succeed in finding and shaping the kind of union that is acceptable to the East as well as to the West. This union is neither pure autocephaly nor absorption, in law or in actual fact, but a sharing of the same faith, the same sacraments, and the spiritual heritage and organization proper to each Church, under the vigilance, both paternal and fraternal, of the successor of him to whom it was said: "Thou art Peter, and upon this rock I will build my Church."

We are hoping that once the union is achieved, there will no longer be a united or uniat Eastern Church but simply an Eastern Church, among whose ranks we ourselves shall re-enter as if we had never departed.[4]

In our age we can distinguish several phases in this mutual rediscovery of East and West.

The first phase runs from 1961 to 1979. During this period Panorthodox Conferences met in Rhodes in 1961, 1963 and 1964. They intensified fraternal communication between the Orthodox Churches, began the process of preparation for a Panorthodox Council, and determined to enter into dialogue with Rome on terms of equality.

This same period saw an increase in the exchange of letters, in meetings, and in reciprocal pilgrimages on the part of the Church of Rome and the Church of Constantinople. On September 20, 1963 Paul VI sent a handwritten letter to Patriarch Athenagoras recognizing him as a brother in the episcopate; the patriarch published the letter in the Bulletin of the Patriarchate under the title: "Two Sister Churches." This was the first time this expression was used in the modern period to describe relations between Rome and Constantinople. This letter and the patriarch's reaction to it made possible the pilgrimage to Jerusalem, three months later, "of the two pilgrims, with their eyes fixed on Christ."[5] December 7, 1965 saw the solemn lifting of the reciprocal excommunications of 1054. In July 1967 Paul VI visited Athenagoras, who in turn visited Rome three months later. In June 1968 the Fourth Panorthodox Conference of Chambesy expressed the hope that all these exchanges might be continued. In February and March 1971 the two letters of Pope Paul VI and Patriarch Athenagoras I represented a first attempt to give theological expression to their experience in their meetings of mutual rediscovery. On December 14, 1975, during the celebration of the tenth anniversary of the lifting of the reciprocal excommunications, Paul VI went on his knees before Metropolitan Meliton, delegate of Patriarch Dimitrios I, successor of Athenagoras, and kissed his feet as a sign of humility and of petition for forgiveness.

The second phase is that of the "dialogue of charity," to use the words spoken by Metropolitan Meliton on November 19, 1964. The Common Declaration issued by Pope John Paul II and Patriarch Dimitrios I on November 30, 1979 shows that the dialogue of charity has opened the way for a theological dialogue and purged the collective memory on both sides. As John Paul phrased it, "it was necessary to create again the context before trying to rewrite the texts together."[6]

The third phase is the phase of theological dialogue, the way for which was being readied since December 1975 by two theological commissions, one Catholic, the other Orthodox, and, since 1977, by a joint committee. On November 30, 1979 John Paul II and Dimitrios I announced, in Istanbul, the creation of a mixed Catholic-Orthodox commission for theological dialogue; it was anticipated that this commission would study the sacraments, the position of the bishop of Rome in the universal Church, the Marian dogmas, and the *Filioque.* Paths to the resolution of differences exist, and the work of the theologians must be accompanied by a constant concern to see what concrete meaning theological progress has for the life of the Churches.

Reconciliations and Rediscoveries within the Western Church

In 1561 the Colloquy of Poissy represented the final abortive attempt at reconciliation prior to the "wars of religion" between the Churches of the Reformation in France and the Roman Church.

In 1541 a colloquy at Regensburg had brought together the Reformers Melanchthon, Bucer and Calvin, and the famous Venetian, Cardinal Gasparo Contarini, one of the most fervent of those evangelical Catholics of the time who were bent on expressing traditional dogma in more accessible formulas. A projected agreement in the form of twenty-three articles was even drawn up, but no definitive conclusion could be reached. This meeting was the last attempt at reconciliation before the Council of Trent.

At that time there were within Catholicism some individuals who were witnesses to ecumenism: for example, in Germany Georg Witzel (1501–1573) and George Cassander (1515–1566), and in France Thomas Copley (1514–1584), an English refugee. It seems that in France the lack of theologians of stature led to politicians taking charge of the effort at reconciliation; thus it was that in 1561 Chancellor Michel de L'Hôpital organized the Colloquy of Poissy which was attended by Theodore Beza, John Calvin's successor at Geneva. The failure of this conference undoubtedly made it possible for Catherine de Medici to turn to the policy of force that led to the massacre of St. Bartholomew's Day, August 24, 1572.

In the seventeenth century ecumenism became the business of specialists, the latter being of two kinds. There were the active intellectuals such as Francis de Sales or Bossuet who wrote an *Exposition de la doctrine de l'Eglise sur les matières de controverse* (Explanation of the Church's Teaching on Points Now Controverted) and who, despite the unfortunate "revocation of the Edict of Nantes" in 1685, was eager to carry on a dialogue with Leibniz the philosopher as well as with Gerhard Wolter of Meulen, Lutheran pastor at Loccum. In 1640, Camus, the bishop of Belley and well known for his literary work, composed *Avoisinement des Protestants vers l'Eglise ro-*

maine (Approach of Protestants to the Roman Church). Then there were the closet intellectuals like the English Benedictine John Barnes (1581–1661), the Oxford scholar Obadrah Walker (1616–1689), the French Benedictine Léandre de Saint-Martin, and the Italian Oratorian Gregorio Panzini, the latter two of whom were sent to England by Urban VIII to gather information.

In the eighteenth century, William Wake, archbishop of Canterbury, and L. E. de Pin and Patrick Piers de Girardin, professors at the Sorbonne, corresponded from 1716 to 1726 for the purpose of bringing about a union between the Anglican and "Gallican" Churches. Cardinal de Noailles corresponded with Count von Zinzendorf (1700–1760), a fervent promoter of pietism whose aim was to restore Christian unity by means of pietist communities that would be spread abroad in the Churches as a leaven of communion.

In the second half of this century revivalist preachers made themselves all things to all men in all the Baptist, Congregationalist, Presbyterian and Methodist communities. According to Fr. Tavard,

> they [the itinerant preachers] prepared Protestantism in the United States for the great ecumenical tasks ahead. In the form of what we now call "evangelicalism" the Pietist return to the sources also left its mark on Anglicanism, giving new vigor to the most Protestant elements in the Church of England. By inspiring a common piety and a common seeking of the Lord through an experiential enjoyment of his gifts, all these movements, though seemingly unconnected with another, kept alive in Protestantism as a whole a vision of Christian unity. When the time came, this vision would take concrete form in particular projects.[7]

In the nineteenth century the revivalist movement was characterized by its emphasis on personal conversion and missionary fervor, and in fact it was in circles dedicated to missionary work that the idea of Christian unity and a reunion of the Churches won most favor and became widespread. In

1806, William Carey, a Baptist missionary, met Henry Martyn, an Anglican missionary, at Serampore in India and proposed that representatives of all the missionaries throughout the world should meet every ten years in Capetown (the Cape of Good Hope would symbolize the hope of Christian unity). Carey was overly optimistic and felt sure that the first such congress could meet in 1810. His expectations were dashed, but missionary zeal henceforth would increasingly feed ecumenical zeal. A shared fidelity in preaching the Gospel was to be felt from that time on, as it is today, to be an important factor in unity.

In 1804 the British and Foreign Bible Society came into existence, its purpose being to bring Protestants and Anglicans together and to promote collaboration among Orthodox, Armenian, Coptic and Syro-Malabar Christians for a dialogue with the non-Christians of the East. The Société des Missions of Paris was formed in 1822; it comprised Lutherans, Reformed and Baptists from France and Switzerland.

In 1824 James Warren Doyle (1786–1834), Catholic bishop of Kildare in Ireland, wrote:

> Conversations between Anglicans and Catholics are a necessity. The present divergence of views is due in most cases to divergent ways of speaking that can in fact be satisfactorily explained, or to ignorance and misunderstandings which have been brought about by ancient prejudices and ill will but which can be overcome. It is pride and points of honor that keep us apart in many areas, and not the love of Christian humility, charity and truth.

The bishop even offered to surrender his episcopal see, without salary, pension or further ambition, if this would promote the union of the Churches.

The year 1846 saw the establishment of the World Evangelical Alliance, which was heavily influenced by revivalist piety and the view that Christians must unite as individuals whatever their ecclesiastical allegiance. The Alliance was an interconfessional organization, and some historians point out that the word "ecumenism" was first used there in its modern sense by the Frenchman, Adolphe Monod. The idea of a world-wide week of prayer was even proposed in the Alliance; on the other hand the Alliance gave evidence of a certain anti-Catholicism and some aversion to any established Church.

The first Young Men's Christian Association was founded in England in 1844, and the first Young Women's Christian Association in France in 1846. While missionary circles were hotbeds of concern for Christian unity, as I pointed out above, groups of young people were no less such. At that time, just as today, young people cannot resign themselves to division among Christians, and they try to shake off the inertia of older generations which are at times more prone to rejecting the impatience of the young than to making themselves docile to the summons of the Spirit which that impatience renders manifest. It is worth calling attention, for example, to the seriousness of the aims set for itself by the Association which had been formed in 1844 at the instigation of George Williams. On June 6 of that year twelve draper's employees formed a group that regarded itself (as Williams' plan put it) as personally united to the Lord Jesus as his disciples, and that was determined to dedicate itself entirely to the extension of Christ's reign among young people. Within a few years similar associations had sprung up in other countries, all of them accepting the program of the London Association.

The World's Alliance of Young Men's Christian Associations (YMCA) was founded in 1878, and the World's Young Women's Christian Association (YWCA) in 1894. These were interconfessional movements of Christian piety that had a universalist basis, the latter being formulated in the famous Paris Basis in 1855 which was meant to provide a common basis for the association of various groups of young people and at the same time make possible a missionary cooperation in accordance with shared principles. The Paris Basis stated: "The Young Men's Christian Associations seek to unite those young men, who, regarding Jesus Christ as their God and Savior, according to the Holy Scriptures, desire to be his disciples, in their doctrine and in their life, and to associate their efforts for the extension of his Kingdom among young men."[8] This declaration contains some important dogmatic assertions. The first of them—"regarding Jesus Christ as their God and Savior according to the Holy Scriptures"—has been retained by many interconfessional and world federations of associations of young people. It has become the basic formula of the Faith and Order Movement and, via this, of the World Council of Churches (beginning in Amsterdam in 1948). The World's YMCA adopted in 1914 a formula with a Trinitarian confession, thus drawing attention to the fact that the Christian faith has for its foundation the mystery of Trinitarian communion; the World Council of Churches gave acknowledgment to this fact in 1961 at New Delhi when it altered the basic formula adopted in 1948 in order to make it explicitly Trinitarian.

In 1895, John Mott (1865–1955), an American, founded the World's Student Christian Federation, which sprang from the Christian Association of Young People in the United States. The Federation had for its purpose to turn students into disciples of Jesus Christ "the only Savior and Lord." The young people from the different denominations thus came to realize that there were disciples of Christ in all the Churches; in their meetings the question of intercommunion quickly came to the fore. Was such intercommunion the ultimate goal of unity, or only a means to a further end? This question, with all the varied responses it evoked, caused suffering and impatience, but it also led to a deepening realization that progress along the road to unity was hardly possible without tackling the problem not only of the Church as such but also of the relations of the Churches among themselves. People also began to realize that the ecumenical movement is one in which the riches of Christianity are to be shared: a testimony to the riches one has received and an acceptance of the riches by which other Christians live.

In 1911 John Mott convened a conference of the World's Student Christian Federation at Constantinople and invited representatives of the Eastern Churches to attend it. This meeting was of decisive importance for the subsequent history of the ecumenical movement, for it gradually became clear that the movement could not be simply Western or pan-Protestant. The contacts and friendships developed at the Constantinople meeting were to make it possible later on for the Russian emigrés who had fled the Revolution of October 1917 to find support in their new adopted countries; as a result of that support they would be able to establish the Institut Saint-Serge and the YMCA publishing house in Paris, the Fellowship of St. Alban and St. Sergius in London, and the St. Vladimir Institute in New York. These organizations played a determining role in the development of ecumenism in the West.

The nineteenth century was also a time of confessional regrouping. It was realized that there was need of reuniting not only individuals but even Churches that had had the same origin but had until now been separated by geography.

The first Lambeth Conference, bringing together all the bishops of the Anglican Communion throughout the world, was held in 1867. Lambeth Palace, which is located in London, beside the Thames and opposite Parliament and Westminster Abbey, is the residence of the archbishop of Canterbury, primate of the Anglican Communion. The first of these conferences which are held every ten years already raised the question of unity. It spoke of "the gift, so rich in blessings, of unity in truth." Its joint letter was addressed "to believers in Jesus Christ, to the priests, deacons and laity of the Church of Christ that is in communion with the Anglican branch of the Catholic Church."

Each of the Lambeth Conferences has made reference to the "Roman" Church. The hope of fruitful dialogue has had its ups and downs. But the Conference of 1908 reminded those present of the thirty-fourth resolution of the 1897 meeting: that "every opportunity be taken to emphasize the Divine purpose of visible unity among Christians, as a fact of revelation."[9]

The Lambeth Conference is not an organ of a centralized

synodal government but a consultative assembly in which the bishops study together the problems facing the entire Anglican Communion in its internal life and in its relations with the other Christian confessions. The Conference makes no binding decisions but composes a letter which expresses the viewpoint of the Anglican Communion on various subjects and makes recommendations regarding a common attitude and common action for the various provinces of the Communion.

The year 1868 saw the initial form of what would become the Lutheran World Federation. The Alliance of Reformed Churches throughout the World was established in 1875; this is an Alliance of those Churches which practice the presbyterian synodal system, in which authority in the Churches is exercised by regional and national synods. In 1881 twenty-eight Churches were represented at the first meeting of the World Methodist Council. In 1889 a conference of Old Catholic bishops was established that has authority over the various Old Catholic National Churches. In 1891 an International Congregational Council met for the first time. In 1905 the Baptist World Alliance was organized.

In 1902 Joachim III, patriarch of Constantinople, and the Holy Synod sent an encyclical letter to all the Orthodox Churches "on the means of a possible reconciliation among those who believe in the true Trinitarian God, in order that the desired day of universal union may come, in accordance with the inscrutable decrees of God." The patriarch envisaged two levels of activity: a union of the Orthodox Churches among themselves, and a solicitude for establishing contact with the non-Orthodox Churches.

At the beginning of the twentieth century, shortly after the law of separation between Church and state, the various unions of Protestant Churches in France showed a desire to form a federation. As early as 1903, at the Synod of the Free Evangelical Churches of Clairac, Wilfrid Monod urged the formation of such a federative organization. The parties had to wait until 1907 for the organization to come into being. One of the main activities of the new Federation was the convocation of a General Assembly; preparations were made for a Constituent Assembly, and this was held at Nîmes in 1909. Ten assemblies followed, usually about every five years, down to that of La Rochelle in 1983. In 1962, at a work session of the Council of the Protestant Federation of France, new statutes were adopted which tend to reflect in a much more comprehensive way the various Churches and movements. Since that time each of the General Assemblies has focused on a theme. For example, the theme at Grenoble in 1969 was: "What kind of development, and for what kind of man?" At Paris in 1975 the theme was: "The Vocation of Protestantism."

The General Assemblies are the supreme organ of the Federation but they have no jurisdiction over their members. They are convoked every three years by the Council and comprise delegates—pastors and laypersons—who are appointed by the member Churches and elected by the movements, societies and institutions. Orthodox and Catholic observers are invited. The Council is made up of members appointed by the Churches and members representing the movements, societies and institutions, and are grouped into departments chosen by the Assembly. The president is elected for three years; the secretary is in charge of administration. The Federation comprises six Churches: the Church of the Augsburg Confession of Alsace and Lorraine (ECAAL), the Lutheran Evangelical Church of France, the Reformed Church of Alsace and Lorraine (ERAL), the Reformed Church of France (ERF), the Federation of Baptist Evangelical Churches of France, and the National Union of Free Evangelical Reformed Churches of France, as well as the Evangelical Mission to the Gypsies and the Popular Mission. The presence of a concordat system in Alsace and Lorraine explains the existence of two Lutheran Churches and two Reformed Churches: those located in Alsace and Lorraine, and those located in the departments of the "interior" where there is no concordat.

The Federation also includes various services, commissions and departments.

In 1908 Spencer Jones and Paul Wattson launched the Octave of Prayer for Unity. Prayer is necessarily at the source of every Christian movement.

N.B. BIRTH AND GROWTH OF THE ECUMENICAL MOVEMENT

A World Missionary Conference was held at Edinburgh, June 13–23, 1910. In his book *The Long Road to Unity* Pastor Marc Boegner, a witness of those events and of everything that followed, writes that the Edinburgh Conference was "the cradle of the ecumenical movement."[10] "In that year," said William Temple, archbishop of Canterbury, "there occurred the most important event in the life of the Church for a generation." The Edinburgh Conference, with John Mott as its president, brought together twelve hundred delegates from the Protestant missions of the entire world. A Chinese delegate, Chêng Ching-yi, uttered the following statement: "You have sent us missionaries who gave us the knowledge of Jesus Christ, and for this we are profoundly grateful to you. But you have also brought us your divisions. We ask you, therefore, to preach only the Gospel to us and to allow Jesus Christ himself to raise up among our peoples, through the action of his Spirit, the Church that meets his norms and that is also in keeping with the character of our race: a Church that will be the Church of Christ in Japan, the Church of Christ in China, in India, and so on. But deliver us from all the 'isms' which you attach to the preaching of the Gospel among us."

The report delivered by Sir Andrew Fraser had already laid heavy emphasis on the great harm done to the proclamation of the good news of salvation by the incredible proliferation of missionary works. These two speeches and the final address of John Mott caused "the participants to enter into themselves" (the first words of Mott's address). Here are some of his further remarks:

> Has it not humbled us increasingly as we have discovered that the greatest hindrance to the expansion of Christianity lies in ourselves? . . . I make bold to say that the Church has not yet seriously attempted to bring the living Christ to all living men. Reality means that we will not only revise our plans concerning the Kingdom, but we will revise with even greater faithfulness the plans with reference to our own lives.[11]

It is not without interest to note that Msgr. Donomelli, bishop of Cremona and personal friend of Pius X, sent a long letter of sympathy to the Conference.

Nine years later, the temporary representative of the Patriarchate of Moscow stated to the Holy Synod: "I think the time has come for the Orthodox Church to examine carefully the problem of the union of the divided Christian Churches. It should study the problem especially in relation to the Anglican, Old Catholic and Armenian Apostolic Churches." There is no thought as yet of the Protestant world or the Roman Catholic world.

In 1920 the Church of Constantinople sent an encyclical letter to all the Churches of the world; its text was: "Love one another earnestly from the heart" (1 Pet 1:22).[12] This appeal emphasizes the need of exchanges and contacts at the practical level but refuses to admit that doctrinal differences will inevitably mean the failure of any attempt to establish a closer unity among the various confessions. It sees in common action the occasion for improved mutual knowledge, the elimination of prejudices, and the creation of a spirit of trust that will militate against disagreements, distrust and proselytism. This document is regarded as of the first importance by historians of the ecumenical movement.

Since that year 1920 a delegation from Istanbul has taken part in the work of an organization which sprang from the new awareness created by Edinburgh. This factual observation brings me to the effects produced by the Edinburgh Conference; as a matter of fact, three movements emerged from it.

The first was the International Missionary Council (1921), with John Mott as its chairman and J. H. Oldham as his assistant. The purpose of the Council was the study, coordination and more harmonious organization of non-Roman Catholic Christian missions. Mott's personal contacts with the Orthodox made it possible to plan a conference to be held in Jerusalem in 1928 on these various objectives.

The second movement was the Stockholm Continuation Committee, which was established on the practical and social bases laid down in the Edinburgh message and which had for its purpose to engage the non-Roman Churches in the study and implementation of the essential documents of the Edinburgh Conference. Nathan Söderblom (1866–1931), Lutheran archbishop of Uppsala, chaired this committee. His entire career had been preparing him for this role. As a student in Paris, a professor at Uppsala and Leipzig, and archbishop, he had become increasingly concerned for the inwardness of faith and for the life into which faith leads the Christian. He therefore stressed five main themes: revelation, the Church, Luther, the cross of Christ, and ecumenical problems. "Nothing left him indifferent; no one felt him to be a stranger." It was due to him that the Life and Work Movement came into existence prior to the 1914–18 war. The first conference of this movement (also known as the "Practical Christianity Movement") was held at Stockholm in 1925.

The Lausanne Continuation Committee traveled the third road leading from Edinburgh. The members of this committee were convinced that authentic Church unity requires a communion in faith and a common doctrine of ministry; they therefore urged the various Churches to study, in their synods, communities, and theological organizations, the problems raised by their doctrinal differences, and to try to overcome these differences. Out of the Lausanne Continuation Committee came the Faith and Order Movement, which held its first conference at Lausanne in 1927. The man chiefly responsible for the Movement was Charles Brent, an Episcopal missionary bishop in the Philippines, for whom Edinburgh had been a great turning point. Of Brent Pastor Marc Boegner writes: "Like so many others of my generation, I am indebted to Bishop Brent for having, as early as the immediate post-Edinburgh period, made me realize the horror of the countless divisions, the shocking rendings of the Lord's coat without seam, but also for having shown me that it is only through love that a way can be found to the visible restoration of the unity of the body of Christ."[13]

There is another important event from this period that must be noted: the Malines Conversations (1921–1926). Two men were responsible for them: an Anglican layman, Lord

Halifax, and a French priest, Fr. Portal. The two men met for the first time in 1890 in Madeira. From then on they continuously visited one another and exchanged ideas on the possibilities of a reunion of the Anglican Communion with the Roman Church. In 1893 they concluded that the first step in a reconciliation of the two Churches would take the form of a re-examination by Rome of the validity of Anglican ordinations. On September 18, 1896 Leo XIII declared that these ordinations "have been and are absolutely null and utterly void." For the time being, this decision put an end to the great hope cherished by Lord Halifax and Fr. Portal.

But then, during the summer of 1920, the two hundred and fifty bishops at the Lambeth Conference made, in the words of Cardinal Gasparri, "one of the most beautiful acts of humility of which I have ever heard." The bishops declared themselves ready to accept from the authorities of the other Churches a form of commission or recognition of their ministry; they even hinted that they were not opposed to some form of "reordination." Halifax immediately wrote to Portal and suggested that they go to Malines and ask Cardinal Mercier if he would agree to organize meetings between two representatives of the two Churches, for the purpose of clearing the air, dissipating misunderstandings, eliminating prejudices on each side, and recovering the historical truth. Five meetings were held (December 6–8, 1921; March 14–15, 1923; November 7–8, 1923; May 19–20, 1925; October 11–12, 1926). Cardinal Mercier died on January 23, 1926, and Fr. Portal passed away on June 20 of the same year. After the departure of these two men the Conversations could not be what they had been.

Is it possible to summarize the results of the Malines Conversations? In the eyes of some the results were negative. Father Rouquette, a Jesuit, wrote in 1966: "The conversations, which looked only to a better mutual knowledge of the two Churches, hindered the dialogue rather than promoted it." And it is in fact possible that certain blunders may have discredited the ecumenical project in the minds of English Catholics, who were unfortunately excluded from conversations which concerned them more than anyone else.

The provisional and seeming failure was due to a twofold delusion: that of the Anglicans, who thought that all of Roman Catholicism was represented by Cardinal Mercier and his friends, and that of the Roman Catholics, who believed that Lord Halifax and his friends represented the whole of Anglicanism. The failure was also due to an unfortunate omission: the English Catholics were not represented at Malines. Yet it was precisely in England that any reconciliation between Catholicism and Anglicanism would have its full meaning and authenticity. The dialogue between Rome and Canterbury could not be a fruitful one unless the Roman Catholic Church in its entirety took part in it.

To other critics, however, the result of the Malines Conversations was positive. The Conversations showed that dialogue is possible between members of the Catholic Church and members of the separated confessions. They also showed that such meetings of limited scope had a greater depth of effectiveness than the great assemblies being held during the same period at Lausanne, Oxford and Stockholm, and that the different types of activity were complementary. The Conversations also illustrated the ecumenical movement's need of prophets and men of initiative, without whose passionate dedication nothing could be undertaken or carried further. Finally, it is a fact that the Conversations confronted Catholic opinion with the question of ecumenism. Above all, they showed the irresistible power of an ecumenical commitment that was wholly based on a spiritual ecumenism: the ecumenism of prayer (recall Fr. Portal and Lord Halifax meditating together on John 17 there above the caminho novo) and the ecumenism of obedience and self-humbling that have been the experience of all true precursors. Thanks to Fr. Portal and Lord Halifax and to their submission to the Spirit, the entire Church in all the individual Churches would one day set out on the new road of ecumenism.

In 1924, in his letter *Equidem verba* to Fidelis von Stotzingen, abbot general of the Benedictines, Pius XI entrusted this Order with the mission of ecumenical contacts with the East. Dom Lambert Beauduin responded to this call as early as 1925 and founded the Priory of Reunion at Amay-sur-Meuse, which was later moved to Chevetogne. In 1926 he started the magazine *Irénikon,* which was devoted chiefly to Orthodox history, liturgy and theology, but was also clearly open to all ecumenical concerns, since if ecumenism is to be authentic it must be global, that is, concerned with all the denominations.

In 1928 Pius XI issued his encyclical *Mortalium animos,* which expressed Rome's misgivings with regard to an ecumenical movement that was still in search of its own proper orientation. The encyclical ratified the Roman refusals of 1918, 1919 and 1921 to take part in the preparation for the Stockholm Conference, as well as the decree of the Holy Office (July 8, 1927) forbidding Catholics to take part in the Faith and Order Conference at Lausanne. The encyclical rejected the ecumenism of that day, not the ecumenism of the present time. One of its effects was to bring Catholic ecumenists to an attitude of prudence: not a human prudence but an entirely spiritual prudence, wholly inspired by a charity that attends only to the movements of the Spirit as it seeks the ways it ought to follow. Roman Catholics would henceforth devote themselves not to meetings, gatherings and spectacular conferences but to the essential task of prayer, theological work, liturgy and hospitality. Such was the vocation accepted by the Priory of Amay-sur-Meuse (soon moved to Chevetogne) and the Centre Istina (the Russian word for "truth") which was founded at Lille in 1932 by Fr. Gomez, transferred to Paris in 1936, and expanded by Fr. Dumont at Boulogne-sur-Seine in 1947 and at the Rue de la Glacière in Paris since 1967.

In 1932, Fr. Paul Couturier, a priest from Lyons, made a retreat at Amay. On his return home he decided to introduce to Lyons the Octave of Prayer for Unity; his efforts were fully supported by Cardinal Gerlier. With the very effective aid of Fr. Villain, a Marist theologian, Fr. Couturier diffused the celebration of the Octave and the idea of spiritual ecumenism; this was a large and decisive achievement. Under the impetus given by Fr. Michalon, the Centre Unité Chrétienne has continued the work of Fr. Couturier. In 1937, Fr. Yves Congar, a Dominican theologian, published a magisterial book which was the first "summa" ever written in such a spirit by a Catholic: *Chrétiens désunis, principes d'un ecuménisme catholique* (*Divided Christendom: A Catholic Study of the Problem of Reunion*, London, 1939).

During the time of Nazi persecution in Germany, Fr. Max Metzger, a Catholic priest, organized a fraternal gathering of separated Christians for purposes of spiritual resistance; their aim was essentially to pray and get others to pray for unity, and to organize exchanges and common activities. In Rome, Fr. Charles Boyer, a Jesuit, founded the Unitas Association, while in France Pastor Marc Boegner, at that time president of the Protestant Federation, popularized the saying of Metropolitan Plato of Kiev: "The walls of separation do not reach up to heaven."

In July 1937 Life and Work held its second conference at Oxford and stated: "Unity does not have its origin in the agreement of human wills but in Jesus Christ whose life permeates his body and subjects all wills to his own." In August 1937 Faith and Order held its conference at Edinburgh and proclaimed that "this unity [of Christians] does not consist in the agreement of our minds or the consent of our wills. It is found in Jesus Christ himself."[14] These two movements had now drawn so close and were so complementary that it was decided in 1938, at Utrecht, to merge them within a World Council of Churches; the establishment of this last was however delayed by the Second World War.

The Constituent Assembly of the World Council of Churches (which numbered one hundred and forty-seven at that point), was held in Amsterdam in 1948. The theme of the gathering was "Man's Disorder and God's Design." The Council adopted a basic text, that is, it defined the nature of the relations which the member Churches were trying to maintain among themselves; in other words, the basic text was a statement of minimal doctrinal agreement. It stated: "The World Council of Churches is a fellowship of churches which accept our Lord Jesus Christ as God and Savior."[15]

The second Assembly was held in Evanston, Illinois in 1954 (one hundred and sixty-three Churches from forty-eight countries) on the theme: "Christ, Sole Hope of the World." The third world gathering was at New Delhi in 1961 on the theme: "Jesus Christ, Light of the World." Some important decisions were made at New Delhi. For one thing, the basic statement was modified to read: "the World Council of Churches is a fellowship of churches which confess the Lord Jesus Christ as God and Savior according to the Scriptures and therefore seek to fulfill together their common calling to the glory of the one God, Father, Son and Holy Spirit."[16] In addition, it was decided to incorporate the International Missionary Council and to admit four major Orthodox Churches (those of Rumania, Poland and Bulgaria, and the Patriarchate of Moscow).

In 1952 the International Catholic Conference on Ecumenical Questions met at Fribourg, Switzerland. The meeting was attended by about fifty theologians, along with the founder of the Conference, Bishop Willebrands, who after the death of Cardinal Bea became president of the Roman Secretariat for Christian Unity that had been established on June 5,1960 after John XXIII's announcement that an Ecumenical Council, Vatican II, was to be held. The official statement published in *L'Osservatore Romano* said of the latter: "The Ecumenical Council does not have for its sole purpose the spiritual welfare of the Christian people; it is also meant as an invitation to the separated Communities to seek the unity for which so many souls long today in all parts of the world."

Non-Catholic observers were invited to the Council in large numbers. Cardinal Bea wrote of them: "They played a decisive role in the working out of the *Decree on Ecumenism.* Their presence at the Council, their participation through prayer, study and the most varied contacts, and the suggestions they offered made the ecumenical problem vividly and deeply real to the bishops." In 1967 the Constitution *Regimini Ecclesiae* on the reform of the Roman Curia made the Roman Secretariat the special office for everything having to do with relations with the other Christian communities. The existence of the Secretariat shows clearly that the Roman Catholic Church is permanently committed to ecumenism.

On December 4, 1965 a ceremony took place at Rome

that had no historical precedent. In Saint Paul outside the Walls the bishops of the Council, the Pope, and a hundred or so delegated observers took part in a liturgical celebration of the word. On January 5 and 6, 1964 Paul VI and Patriarch Athenagoras met in Jerusalem on a common pilgrimage. In a joint statement they said: "The two pilgrims, with their eyes fixed on Christ, the Exemplar and Author with the Father of unity and peace, pray to God that this meeting may be the sign and prelude of things to come for the glory of God and the illumination of his faithful people."[17] On July 25, 1967 the two men met again in Constantinople when the Pope visited it, and a third time in Rome, on October 26 of the same year, when the Pope received the patriarch at St. Peter's.

In 1965 the non-Chalcedonian Churches (cf. above, Chapter 1, on the separation of the Semitic Churches) met for joint conversations at Addis Ababa. In March 1966 contact was officially restored between the Anglican Communion and the Roman Catholic Church at the historic meeting in Rome of Dr. Ramsey, archbishop of Canterbury, and Pope Paul VI. In April 1967 the Anglican primate again visited both the Catholic Church and the Protestant Federation of France. In February 1970 Cardinal Marty returned this visit in the name of the French episcopate. A dialogue between Roman Catholics and Old Catholics was opened on November 7, 1966 when a joint letter signed by the bishops of each confession was read in all the parish churches of both confessions. The Greek Orthodox and the Lutheran World Federation were in contact February 25–28, 1967.

The Fourth Assembly of the World Council of Churches was held at Uppsala in July 1968 on the theme: "Behold, I make all things new," which expressed the essential object of Christian hope. At this meeting the question was raised in forthright terms of the possible entrance of the Roman Catholic Church into the World Council of Churches. Paul VI gave an answer to this question when he visited the headquarters of the World Council of Churches in Geneva in June 1969: "In fraternal frankness we do not consider that the question of the membership of the Catholic Church in the World Council is so mature that a positive answer could or should be given."[18]

Whatever be the case with the membership of the Roman Catholic Church in the World Council of Churches, the point that needs to be emphasized here is the active collaboration between the Secretariat for Unity in Rome and the World Council, and, in the field, the involvement of Christians from the various Churches in different areas of activity: theological, pastoral, spiritual, practical. This collaboration is becoming increasingly close, thanks to the Joint Working Group of the Roman Catholic Church and the World Council of Churches, but thanks above all to Faith and Order.

The Fifth Assembly of the World Council was held in Nairobi, Kenya from November 23 to December 10, 1975, on the theme: "Jesus Christ Frees and Unites." The delegates from two hundred and eighty-six Anglican, Orthodox and Protestant Churches examined the implications of unity and liberation in Jesus Christ for the life of the Church and the world. Some Catholic observer delegates took part in this. There was further discussion of the conciliarity of "conciliar fellowship" (cf. Chapter III). This represented an advance in regard to the question of unity.

The Sixth Assembly was held at Vancouver, Canada, from July 24 to August 10, 1982. The main theme, "Jesus Christ, Life of the World," was subdivided into four other themes: Life as God's Gift, Life Victorious over Death, Life in Its Fullness, and Life in Unity. Three hundred and one Churches (in one hundred countries) that are presently members of the World Council took part in the preparation for the Assembly.

On Pentecost 1982 the presidents of the World Council of Churches spoke as follows in their message:

> It is interesting to note that "they were all together in one place" when the gift of the Spirit came. Does this not mean that in order to receive the gifts of the Spirit in their fullness the Churches must come together? This is what we have been allowed to experience in the ecumenical movement.

As the presidents of the World Council of Churches we want to bear witness to this reality. In the ecumenical movement each tradition brings its treasures to our common worship and work—the ancient glory of Orthodox liturgy, the joy of Spirit-filled hymns, the biblical depth of devout Protestants, the beauty and order of Anglican worship. More and more also our Roman Catholic brothers and sisters contribute to this common life. In sharing their gifts with one another, the Churches have been renewed through the power of the Holy Spirit.[19]

III.

ECUMENICAL LIFE TODAY

Common Christian Witness

Nowadays ecumenism is hardly front-page news for the mass-circulation magazines. Is it therefore dead? By no means! The ecumenical life has quite simply changed its character; it has become diversified and widespread, with the result that it has also become commonplace. It is now lived day by day and passes through the multitude of unobtrusive but effective small changes that are practically imperceptible to those who are alert only to the dramatic and sensational. These small changes and embodiments are daily renewing the bonds between the Churches and gradually restoring the experience of communion. In many places the people "at the base" practice throughout the year a "practical ecumenism," an ecumenism of common action and common Christian witness, for the "unmerited gift [of unity] requires that witness be borne in common."[1] That is precisely what the *Decree on Ecumenism* of Vatican II urges on all Christians:

> Before the whole world let all Christians confess their faith
> in God, one and three, in the incarnate Son of God, our Re-
> deemer and Lord. United in their efforts, and with mutual
> respect, let them bear witness to our common hope which
> does not play us false. . . . Cooperation among Christians viv-
> idly expresses that bond that already unites them.[2]

57

Common Christian witness can take many forms. There is, for example, concrete involvement in Christian efforts to abolish torture, in caritative and social activities, and in the common assertion of hope that was proclaimed by the Faith and Order Conference at Bangalore in 1978.[3] Christians, who not too long ago were squared off against each other, now find themselves working shoulder to shoulder to serve their brothers and sisters, to the point even of dying for them, and this at times as the result of torture.

And yet as our ecumenical activity expands and intensifies, we renew the experience of those who have preceded us on the journey to unity. If the one Church is to become the Church God wants, it is not enough to establish an interecclesial network of solidarity in action. For that which divides the Churches is, at least in large measure, and especially so since the sixteenth century, of the doctrinal order. In the ecumenical movement we cannot simply respect and love one another; rather, aided by fraternal communion in a love that is centered on Jesus Christ and in an obedience, based on his, to the Father's will, we must supply what is still lacking in our full acceptance of all the means of salvation. We must help one another as Christian brothers and sisters to become together what God wants us to be, by receiving and giving to one another with "the right hand of fellowship" (Gal 2:9). There is a tension between the truth of love and the love of truth, between the requirements of charity and the requirements of faith. Consequently there is need of a doctrinal dialogue.

Doctrinal Dialogue

For a long time now the ecumenical movement has given rise to dialogue among Christians as they rediscover themselves to be brothers and sisters desirous of mutual knowledge and understanding and as they therefore quickly decide to focus on questions of faith. According to Fr. Congar:

> Catholics and their theologians lived for a long time in a closed universe. The drawbridges used indeed to be lowered so that others might enter in, but the questions and

ideas of these others hardly penetrated into the enclosure. Today isolation has become impossible. It is characteristic of our world that everyone is present to everyone else thanks to the communications media. Due to the meeting and commingling of ideas and to the pluralism that has become the environing situation . . . dialogue . . . has acquired a comprehensive value that extends beyond the value associated with dialogue in the narrow sense of an exchange of ideas. Dialogue now signifies the overall attitude of one for whom others exist as people to whom he can give something and from whom he can receive something.[4]

Ever since the Council the Catholic Church has officially and resolutely committed itself to dialogue in accordance with the principles set down in the Decree *Unitatis redintegratio* on ecumenism (nos. 5–12). Examples of dialogue are many and varied, and are to be found at the international and national or regional levels. Some are official; others are unofficial or private, as, for example, the Dombes Group in France.

The work of theologians is progressing and being refined with the help of consultations and of publications that submit initial essays in convergence to constructive criticism. This kind of work is making it gradually possible to dismantle the walls of mutual misunderstanding and prejudice, and is leading to the surprised realization that what unites us is infinitely more important than what separates us. I am not able here to give a list of the various commissions or to catalogue the contents of their work and the themes studied therein, but I have provided such a list and catalogue elsewhere in great detail.[5] At this point I would like simply to suggest the method followed in all these dialogues, which are seeking to restore unity by achieving unanimity in the Christian faith ("unanimity" is not the same as "uniformity" in theological expression). The method is that of the dialogue of prayer and charity; the most illustrious example of such a dialogue since Vatican II has been given us by Patriarch Athenagoras and Pope Paul VI.

There was a time when Christians on both sides learned our catechism "against" some one and asserted our doctrine "against" some one. The age of controversial theology is now past. Controversy and polemics used to harden respective positions and strengthen the contesting parties with more or less unconscious self-justifications; they patterned the level of theological positions, where legitimate diversity is really possible, after the level of the affirmations of faith, where unanimity is required. In other words, and more clearly, controversy and polemics too often caused a mere theological position or Scholastic opinion to be presented as essential to the affirmation of the truth of faith. Nowadays, however, spiritual ecumenism and the spirit of fraternal love and mutual good will—everything that St. Paul calls upon the Christians of Ephesus to be in their relations with one another (Eph 4)—inspire all these dialogues and promote a better approach to the truth by sweeping away all the false problems and giving a proper appreciation of cultural and historical traditions in such diverse areas as religious affectivity, liturgical life, spirituality, and theological thematization.

Reference back to the tradition of the undivided Church of the Fathers is proving especially fruitful in the doctrinal dialogue. A knowledge of history also makes it possible to situate better and thus relativize certain facts and questions and to discern with clarity the relation between the language faith uses and the reality intended by the language. It also becomes possible for us to free ourselves from the iron collar of expressions and formulations that are too polemic in their overtones, and to engage in a common search (admittedly, always a difficult and risky undertaking) for a new language that will speak to the man of our time. Here, in fact, we have one of the things contemporary ecumenism is seeking: a common confession of faith.[6]

Catholics working the field of ecumenical theology have been especially helped by a principle of which the Council has reminded us: the principle that "in Catholic doctrine there exists an order or 'hierarchy' of truths, since they vary in their relation to the foundation of the Christian faith."[7] Oscar Cullmann has said that this statement is "the most important point made in the Decree and the one most revolutionary in its effect on the future of the dialogue."[8] In accordance with the wishes of Paul VI, the same point is more fully developed in the *Directory Concerning Ecumenical Matters*, Part 2, Section II, 5,[9] and again in the document entitled *Reflections and Suggestions Concerning Ecumenical Dialogue*, Section IV, 4b.[10] The Declaration *Mysterium Ecclesiae*, Sections 4 and 5, takes up two points which provide a solid foundation on which to reformulate the Christian faith and make it meaningful to our contemporaries.[11]

Another principle that is applied in dialogue, especially by the French-speaking Dombes Group, is what Fr. de Bacicchi has called

> the principle of "dogmatic concentration." In our joint spiritual contemplation of Christ and his truth we realize that the solution of conflicts comes through the purification and correction of one-sided and partial views and through the integration of the data which are in tension. The aim is to do justice to all the basic and imprescriptible requirements within a common truth that lies not behind us but ahead of us, and within a Christianity that is purer, more demanding spiritually and intellectually, and more balanced as well.[12]

But as the doctrinal dialogue progresses and time passes, we become aware that it faces a challenge. The challenge which this ecumenical work—but also the conciliar work of Vatican II itself—must meet is that of "reception." I refer to the process, which is a properly ecclesiological one, by which the ecclesial body progressively makes its own a decision which initially it did not accept; it does this by gradually coming to see the measure promulgated as one truly in keeping with its life. This process is not an easy one. The temptation very often exists either of assigning priority to those elements that define the confession, or of seeking compromises which will make it possible to retain these elements in the common declaration. But both of these attitudes represent a refusal of conversion. When doctrinal agreements have been worked out, the response to them is too often an attempt to find therein the whole of the confessional faith, including points rendered explicit after the original breaks that make such agreements a necessity now. Yet, as Fr. Tillard has observed, "the attempt from the outset to demand that reconciliation between the Churches meet conditions of plenitude really means the smothering of any hope that a conciliar fellowship may one day come into existence."[13]

In our effort to win acceptance and understanding for the process whereby the results of dialogues and the dialogue method itself are "received," we have perhaps not yet made good use of the examples which the history of dogma offers us in this area. The study of this history shows us that the Fathers of the Church and the Councils practiced an "economy." What does economy mean in this context? St. Eulogius, patriarch of Constantinople and friend of Pope St. Gregory the Great, gives an explanation for which he appeals to St. Athanasius, the first to practice this economy, and to St. Gregory Nazianzus. According to Eulogius, the practice of economy means that "when the dogmas of the Church are well established but are expressed in different ways, we agree to say nothing about certain words, especially if these words are not a source of serious scandal for those whose intention is sufficiently upright."[14]

The Cappadocian Fathers and, chief among them, St. Basil made use of this economy. Why? They knew from experience the difficulties caused by the word *homoousios* which the Council of Nicaea (325) had used to express the identity of nature in Son and Father. Any demand that the same term be applied to the Holy Spirit might well give rise to, or revive, endless disputes. For this reason, though convinced that the term was indeed applicable to the Holy Spirit, St. Basil wrote his fine treatise on the Holy Spirit without ever saying in so many words that the Holy Spirit is God and is consubstantial with the Father and the Son. And yet the whole of his treatises moves the reader to this certainty. Furthermore—still in the spirit of economy—Basil preferred to express the faith while using the words of Scripture and avoiding any not found there, even if they had the same meaning as the words of Scripture.

He explained this practice to the monks for whom he drew up a confession of the orthodox faith, and made the point that when there is need of expressing our opposition to heresy, we must not hesitate to use words (such as *homoousios*) which are not in Scripture.[15]

In 381 the Council of Constantinople confessed the true faith in the Spirit, and yet it adopted a Creed that demonstrates the same economy practiced by St. Basil and the Cappadocians. The Creed of Nicaea had ended with "and [we believe] in the Holy Spirit." This Creed then became the Nicaeno-Constantinopolitan creed, which is professed by all Christians despite their divisions, through the addition of: "the Lord and Giver of life, who proceeds from the Father and together with the Father and the Son is worshiped and glorified, and who has spoken through the prophets." The Council of Cosntantinople states only implicitly, and not explicitly, that the Holy Spirit is God and is "consubstantial." This method won the approval of the early Fathers. Severus of Antioch remarks that "the Council did not say that the Holy Spirit is God or that he is consubstantial, lest it alienate those with sick ears,"[16] those whose faith was correct but who were shocked at hearing terms used to which they were not accustomed.

Paul VI likewise called attention to, and approved, this recourse to economy:

> And here, too, charity must come to our aid, as it helped Hilary and Athanasius to recognize the sameness of faith underlying the differences of vocabulary as a time when serious disagreements were creating divisions among Christian bishops. Did not pastoral love prompt St. Basil, in his defense of the true faith in the Holy Spirit, to refrain from using certain terms which, accurate though they were, could have given rise to scandal in one part of the Christian people? And did not St. Cyril of Alexandria consent in 433 to abandon his beautiful formulation of theology in the interests of making peace with John of Antioch, once he had satisfied himself that in spite of divergent modes of expression, their faith was identical?[17]

History shows that the method applied at Constantinople was successful. It would be profitable for us to adopt it in connection with the process whereby the results of theological dialogues are received, in order that these dialogues too may be successful. "Genuine doctrinal ecumenism," Msgr. Nédoncelle used to say, "consists in thinking that no one has yet gained a complete knowledge of God's revelation in Jesus Christ."[18] The Council, too, has emphasized this aspect of faith. The process of reception is not yet complete; it will be subject to delays and calls for patience. Time, a great deal of time, is required for mentalities to be altered, minds to change, memories to be purified.

Spiritual Ecumenism

All forms of ecumenism draw their life-giving nourishment from the wellsprings of the Spirit. They are steeped in the prayer of Jesus for unity, which the Spirit puts in the hearts and on the lips of the millions of men and women gathered together in which Fr. Couturier and Fr. Maurice Villain used to call "the invisible monastery" that is given an abiding visible form in monastic and religious communities.

The annual Week of Prayer for Unity (January 18–25) is a time of intense prayer for reunion, but it is not the only time; in many places and in many hearts this Week of Prayer is a week of three hundred and sixty-five days. In view of the riches and progress of ecumenical experience this prayer becomes one of praise and thanksgiving for the gift already received and lived out. It also is a prayer of invocation, intercession, supplication and repentance in view of what has not yet been received and lived out. God grant that the annual celebration of Unity Week not reflect an ecumenism of drawbridges lowered for a few days or even only a few hours a year, by Churches and communities that continue to exist as fortresses lined up against one another!

The role of spiritual ecumenism is basic. Theological dialogue as a practical activity requires spiritual preparation in the Churches and a spiritual reception in order that what is theologically possible may also become really possible at every level in the life of the Churches and communities. For, as Joseph Ratzinger has insisted, "what is theologically possible may be wasted by spiritual attitudes and thus become theologically impossible once again; but what is theologically possible may also become spiritually possible and thereby acquire a greater theological depth and purity."[19]

PROGRESS

These many threads of contemporary ecumenical life are gradually being woven together to form a people of God that has overcome its divisions. There is no question as yet of full communion, but there is indeed an increasingly intimate association that reflects a radical conversion of mentalities and forms of behavior.

In the past, the dynamism at work was that of separation, hatred and scorn, all of them works of Satan the divider; the dynamism operative today is the dynamism of communion, reconciliation, and encounter, all fruits of the Spirit. In the past, divided Christians used to think: "We are first and foremost in a state of separation, although a certain Christian substance still joins us together." Today "the experience of the new generations is quite different: they are conscious not of disunion but of union, not of what separates but of what unites. . . . This is a new experience, a new datum to which theology must respond" (P. Duprey). This new experience urges Christians to do everything possible together and to give concrete expression to such unity as has already been recovered. And did not Pope Paul VI speak of the separated brethren as "those with whom our communion is not yet complete" (Easter Message, 1973)? And in fact the *Decree on Ecumenism* speaks rather of brethren who are "distant" (*sejuncti*) rather than simply "separated" (*separati*).

This increasingly intimate association should not be allowed to deceive us. There are decisive steps still to be taken if we are to reach full communion and unity. But all that has been achieved or is now being achieved is what turns ecumenism into living flesh and blood. Without these achievements the ecumenical movement would be in danger of being only a set of intellectual problems for theologians, a set of negotiations among authorities and people in charge. Yet the movement is evidently the Spirit acting in the entire people of God as they undergo a conversion through all the spiritual, theological and practical advances that are themselves precisely fruits of the Spirit.

It is sometimes thought stylish to talk of stagnation. Admittedly, the ten or fifteen years that followed upon Vatican II were marked by extraordinary enthusiasm and hope. So much happened which would have been unthinkable only a few years before that there seemed to be reason, humanly speaking, for thinking unity to be within reach and bound to come within a generation. Today we realize that the road to unity is likely to be a very long one still. A certain amount of "settling" is therefore inevitable. But the essential thing is to be found elsewhere: in the promise-filled reality of a movement that originates in the Spirit. And this movement has even advanced so far that we find ourselves now inquiring about models of unity or the form which our recovered unity may take. I shall return to this point further on.

In Doctrinal Ecumenism

These advances are fruits of the Spirit attained through the dialogues of the very numerous commissions or joint working groups—international or national, official or private— which I listed, along with the documents they have published, at the end of my book on the various dialogues.[20]

According to the survey made by Ehrenstrom and Gassmann,[21] about twenty main themes have been discussed: the Gospel (Scripture and tradition), the creeds and confessions of faith, the development of doctrine, the Holy Spirit, Christ, spirituality and worship, salvation, holiness, the Church and the world, baptism, the Eucharist, apostolic succession, ministry and priesthood, the episcopate, the papacy, the authority of the Church, women in the Church, mixed marriages, the Church and society, and unity. J. Puglisi has published a list of bibliographies for the study of the various dialogues; this has been regularly updated by the bulletin of the *Centro pro Unione* in Rome and presently contains 2,587 entries on ninety-two dialogues.[22]

The Theological Dialogue Between the Churches of the West (Catholic Church, Reformation Churches, Anglican Communion). This dialogue has shown real progress by comparison with the dialogue between the Churches of the East and the West; this is a rather paradoxical fact, given the matters in dispute between the Churches of the West. The dialogue among the latter rarely focuses on the fundamental articles of the symbol of faith, Trinity and Christology, since these are regarded by the participants as settled matters. The debate on justification by faith now seems essentially finished, even if the theological expressions of this truth remain divergent and it is possible for the theologians to be critical of certain systematizations of it. The dialogue is concerned primarily with questions of ecclesiology and sacramental theology: the mystery and structure of the Church, Gospel and Church ("Scripture and tradition"), Spirit and Church, apostolicity and the unity of the Church, authority in the Church (the episcopate), the social teaching of the Church, etc.; baptism, Eucharist (including the difficult question of eucharistic hospitality), ministries and ordination (priesthood), marriage. More recently there has been a tendency to tackle the problem of the ministry of unity in the Church universal.[23] One rather remarkable phenomenon is the convergence of the themes discussed in different and independent dialogues: for example, the pattern in the Anglican-Roman Catholic International Commission (ARCIC) has been fully parallel to that of the Dombes Group, although (as I can attest) there has been no communication between the participants of the two groups. ARCIC, established in 1966 by Paul VI and Archbishop Ramsey, reported on the overall progress of its work in a recent document.[24]

The themes on which the most decisive progress has been made are these: the relation between Gospel and Church, which means also between Scripture and tradition; the apostolicity of the Church and of the sacraments. There is general acceptance of the validity of baptisms in the major confessions. The biblical and traditional idea of a memorial sacrifice has made possible a friendly approach to the relation between the Eucharist and the mystery of the cross as the once-and-for-all sacrifice of Christ. A heightened appreciation of the epiclesis has made possible a better understanding of the Real Presence. The main problem in this area, as far as Protestants and Catholics are concerned, is that of the permanence of this Presence after the celebration. In the area of ministry, there is a growing convergence on several points; the structural function of the ordained ministry in the Church, its apostolicity, and the Spirit's gift to the Church which ministry represents are all matters on which there is a growing agreement. Even the episcopate is today becoming the object of very searching ecumenical reflection. It is a fact, nonetheless, that, as I shall say further on, the question of ministries is still the most serious obstacle on the road to full communion, although it is less of an obstacle today than in the past and will become less of an obstacle tomorrow than it is today.

Dialogues between the Catholic Church and the Orthodox Church. On the occasion of the seventh centenary of the Council of Lyons (1274), Pope Paul wrote Cardinal Willebrands, his legate, a letter which is very important from the ecclesiological standpoint. In it, he attributes the failure of what he calls "the sixth of the general synods held in the West" to a failure to accept pluralism in the expression of the faith. Also lacking in the past was the "dialogue of charity" (to use the fine expression of Metropolitan Meliton) which Paul VI and his brother, Patriarch Athenagoras, inaugurated.

On September 20, 1963 Paul VI sent the patriarch a handwritten letter that exerted a profound influence in the East. When the letter was published in the bulletin of the patriarchate it carried the title: "Two Sister-Churches." This was the first time that this term was used in modern times to characterize relations between the two Churches of Rome and Constantinople. The letter and the reaction in the patriarchate created the necessary ecclesiological presuppositions and made possible the meeting of the two men in Jerusalem. In

July 1967, during his visit to Istanbul-Constantinople, Paul VI developed this ecclesiology of the sister-Churches and explicitly acknowledged that Orthodox and Catholics belong to the same Church and that the division between them is therefore located within the one Church of Christ. The two hierarchies are in charge of a single flock.

In his letter of February 8, 1971 Paul VI did not hesitate to write that an "almost total communion" already existed between the two sisters, and on March 21 Athenagoras answered that "they are indeed not estranged in their communion in the mystery of the man-God Jesus and of his humano-divine Church." The patriarch justifies this assertion of communion in Christ by the fact that "the two Churches have never ceased to recognize the validity of the apostolic priesthood in the other and of the sacrament of the divine Eucharist as celebrated by the other."

On December 14, 1975 Patriarch Dimitrios I announced to the Pope that he had made up his mind "to further this holy cause of sacred ties with Rome and to effect a passage from the dialogue of love to preparations, always marked by love, for a theological dialogue" in accordance with the Holy Synod and an interorthodox consultative group. As everyone knows, on that same day, during the celebration of the tenth anniversary of the lifting of the reciprocal excommunications of 1054, Paul VI kissed the feet of the patriarch's envoy, Metropolitan Meliton.

On November 30, 1979 Pope John Paul II and Patriarch Dimitrios announced the opening of the dialogue and the appointment of a mixed commission. The themes suggested for the commission's consideration: the sacraments, the place of the bishop of Rome in the universal Church, the Marian dogmas and the *Filioque*. As far as concerns the ministry of the Church of Rome and its bishop in the universal Church, it is worth recalling here these statements of theologian Joseph Ratzinger:

> Rome should not require anything more on this point than
> was found in the formularies and practice of the first millen-

nium. When, during the Pope's visit to St. George's Cathedral in Phanar, on July 25, 1967, Patriarch Athenagoras spoke of the Pope as "the successor of Peter, the first in honor among us, the one who presides over the community of love," the words of this great Church leader conveyed the substance of what had been said about the primacy during the first millennium, and Rome should not ask for anything more.[25]

The dialogue between the Catholic Church and the pre-Chalcedonian Churches led to common declarations of Paul VI and the Syrian Patriarch Mar Ignatius Jacob III in October 1971 and of Paul VI and Coptic Patriarch Amba Shenouda III in May 1973, to the effect that "there is no difference in the faith they profess concerning the mystery of the Word of God made flesh and become really man."[26]

A dialogue was begun in 1967 between the Russian Orthodox Church and the Catholic Church. There have thus far been five conversations, and progress has been made on the following subjects: the role of Christians in society; local Churches and the universal Church.

Progress in Several Areas. One of the most spectacular advances has undoubtedly been the French *Traduction oecuménique de la Bible* (Ecumenical Translation of the Bible), which has been followed by similar translations in many other languages. The joint work done by exegetes from different Churches both in establishing the text and in composing the notes undoubtedly amounts to a common act of faith. Need I remind the reader that French-speaking peoples can now pray the Our Father together in the same translation? Honesty compels one to admit, however, that an attempt to secure an ecumenical translation of the Apostles' Creed and the Nicaeno-Constantinopolitan Creed failed some years back, the stumbling block being the expression "Catholic Church."

Another advance that needs to be emphasized is the search for common professions and confessions of faith. Christians are increasingly aware of their common responsibility for a common proclamation of the Gospel to the men and women of our times. This common task requires of Christians that they move beyond their divisions, be converted to the essentials of the faith, and present this faith in a manner adapted to the different cultures in today's world.

Progress made in regard to the theme and reality of unity has likewise been remarkable. It concerns two points: the unity that is to be sought, and models of unity.

The *unity to be sought* is not uniformity. It does not require a standardization of organizational forms and of liturgical, spiritual and theological traditions, or in short, of all that gives the seamless robe of Christ its many colors. Better still, the only authentic unity that is "catholic" in the ancient and not in the confessional sense of the word allows room for legitimate differences. As J.A. Moehler observed in the nineteenth century, "unity and divergence in the two aspects of Christianity that are under discussion here have their basis in the Church itself, since they represent two different states of the Church. This explains their unity in diversity and at the same time shows us how they can be and ought to be in harmony." Further on, the same writer offers this indictment of sectarian heresy: "Being unable to tolerate differences. . . . A simple difference is a difference precisely in relation to another with which it co-exists within the same unity."[27] The whole problem is to discern accurately and in common what is of the order of unanimity and unity and what of the order of legitimate differences.

The second area of progress in regard to the concept and reality of unity has to do with the *models of unity.* Let me try to describe briefly the state of ecumenical thinking on this subject.

The Holy Spirit who has been guiding us along the road to full unity has cleared this road of a certain number of prejudices and outdated disputes. He, then, is the "source of our communion" and "activator of the ecumenical movement," to use expressions of Paul VI.[28] Through the Spirit we are already in a mysterious way the children of God and brothers and sisters in Jesus Christ. The reality of the eschaton is already present in the lives of human beings and of the world and is awaiting the moment when Christ reaches his full stature and the number of the elect is complete. Then we shall be "a people brought into unity from the unity of the Father, the Son and the Holy Spirit," to use the words of St. Cyprian that are cited by Vatican II's *Constitution on the Church*.[29] Such is the unity toward which the ecumenical movement is advancing. But as we wait for that fulfillment, all those who live in communion with God and with their brothers and sisters ought to form an ecclesial communion as well—and that is our problem. Even if this communion is by its nature invisible, because it exists in faith and at the level of mystery, it should also manifest itself visibly and bear witness to the world that the Father really sent his Son and that the Son handed himself over in order to gather the scattered children of God (Jn 11:52). More than that, this visible unity ought to serve the entire world as the sign that arouses faith in Jesus Christ (Jn 17).

This certitude of faith has now become a common possession and has stimulated all the recent ecumenical investigations of unity and the forms unity can take. At the Assembly of the World Council of Churches in New Delhi (1961) the emphasis was on the fact that visible unity is local unity. At the Uppsala Assembly (1968) it was added that visible unity is diversified unity. Since 1968 an effort has been made to take greater account of an aspect already brought out by New Delhi which emphasized not only local unity but also the entire Christian community of all places and times. An effort has also been made to respond to the call issued at Uppsala: to work toward the time when "a genuinely universal council can finally speak in the name of all Christians." This openness to universality was accompanied by extensive reflection on the theme and reality of conciliar fellowship.

The Faith and Order Commission took up and continued the study of this subject: at Louvain (1971) it made an effort to describe the unity we seek as that of a "conciliar fellowship."[30] The Salamanca Colloquium (1973) on "Concepts of Unity and Models of Union" approved this idea. It is important that we properly understand the notion of "conciliar fellowship" because it is currently used in ecumenical talk; at the same time, however, it is explained in different ways. In addition, the word "council," which in English can mean either "assembly" or "administrative or executive body" or "deliberations [of such a body]," adds to the imprecision. In the Nairobi Report (1975) it is said in Section II ("What Unity Requires") that "the one Church is to be envisioned as a conciliar fellowship of local churches which are themselves truly united."[31] At Chantilly (April 1977) H. Meyer explained this passage as follows:"In this 'conciliar fellowship' the various local Churches recognize one another as part of the same Church of Christ and as practicing a total communion among themselves with regard to baptism, the Eucharist, ministry, witness, and service." Meyer adds: "There is no question, however, of a monolithic unity (cf. Nairobi, no. 4). The 'conciliar fellowship' is marked by a diversity which we should not only tolerate but actively seek."[32]

During the same meeting at Chantilly Fr. Pierre Duprey said that in his view this description of unity represented an important advance and that as Catholics we can accept this framework and perspective, provided that one and the same faith is proposed by the Churches entering the fellowship. He observed, in addition, that since Vatican II the Catholic Church has been paying new attention to an ecclesiology of communion and that the intuition being developed there is partly the same as the one behind "conciliar fellowship."

Here, then, there are convergences—remote but fruitful—that can be greeted as a sign of the Spirit. Fr. Duprey made a further important remark:

> We will perhaps have to find intermediate forms because we will not be able to reach in a single step the model of union that would most effectively show us to be truly a single community. Among these intermediate forms there is one that is widespread throughout the world but unfamiliar to us Catholics: I mean "Councils of Churches" and "Christian Councils," which are something different from what we are here calling "conciliar fellowship."

In what does the difference consist? As seen in a Catholic perspective, "conciliar fellowship" is based on a community of faith and sacramental life, even though the expressions of faith and the modalities of ecclesial life may be different. A "Council of Churches," on the other hand, is made up of delegates from the Churches which are in their present state of diversity and divergence. A "Christian Council" covers an even broader area and can include Christian organisms that are not Churches.

These Councils fit the definition which the World Council of Churches gave of itself at Nairobi: "The World Council of Churches is constituted for the following function[s] and purpose[s] . . . to call the Churches to the goal of visible unity in one faith and in one eucharistic fellowship expressed in worship and in common life in Christ, and to advance toward that unity in order that the world may believe."[33] The role of a Council, then, is to call for unity but not to establish it, to organize the joint actions which play an important role in, for example, the life of the World Council of Churches but not to launch doctrinal dialogues. The importance of such Councils is clear: they are an effective means of helping Churches enter into dialogue and bringing them gradually toward a real "conciliar fellowship."

The purpose of the ecumenical movement is thus clear to all. Unity among all the Christian communions has not been completely lost, but it still needs to be recovered and completed. The goal can only be visible unity in a faith that finds expression in a variety of formulations and in communion in a single Eucharist, and this within an organic body which, however, tolerates various types of organization. This kind of diversity in unity must be animated by witness and by Christian service in the world, so that the liberation of human beings in Jesus Christ may be effectively proclaimed to them. This visible unity, which is the work of the Spirit, can only be attained through the gradual re-establishment of communion among the Churches.

In Concrete Ecumenism

We have come to understand with increasing clarity that while visible unity is indeed the goal of the ecumenical movement, it is a unity that can be made real only in the concrete situations of the human race. Commitment to unity and commitment to mission are inseparable, especially when the mission is understood as a sharing in the efforts of men and women to build the new world which God wants. The restoration of unity among Christians and the service given to human hopes are thus to be seen as the two sides of a single calling: the calling to be genuine instruments of the gospel and servants of God's plan. Only a Church that is truly one can be the authentic sign of hope which the human race needs. A common commitment to the service of human hopes is one of the most powerful means of re-establishing communion among Christians; in other words, theological ecumenism and practical ecumenism go together, and the bond between them is welded in spiritual ecumenism, in the prayer of Jesus that unity may exist so that the world will believe him to be the Savior sent by the Father.

Like martyrdom—which reflects God's power in man, is a fuller confession of Christ in the Spirit than a simple profession of the creed is, and is a reality in our day—a common practice of evangelical commitment to the service of human beings can be a fuller expression of our common faith than a doctrinal agreement pure and simple. Practice, when truly inspired by charity (*agape*), makes the truth and manifests it as well. Furthermore, it is highly significant that Christians from the various confessions who are jointly involved in the service of their brothers and sisters feel more united with one another in Christ than they do with members of their own Church. There is a shared perception of the presence of Christ's grace and an acknowledgement of shared experience. The Holy Spirit, in calling Christians and their Churches to a common witness, casts them into the crucible in which unity can be rewelded. But it is not enough for individuals to feel and declare themselves reunited; the Churches as such must also enter into communion. The *koinonia* must be sealed in an organic manner; unity must take visible form so that it can be seen. Theological reflection must make the whole dimension of common witness an integral part of its considerations on unity by show-

ing how this witness leads to a common reading and confession
of the one faith and to a common adherence to the one Lord.
Christian witness, for its part, must take into account the requirements to which theological reflection leads.

Progress at the level of concrete ecumenism is not only a
matter of deepening the relation and interdependence between theology and common action. It is also achieved
through a multitude of formal and informal undertakings, institutional or non-institutional exchanges, and spiritual meetings. Here are some examples: the joint programs of Cimade,
of the Catholic Committee against World Hunger and for Development, and of Catholic Welfare; the Ecumenical Association of Christians for the Abolition of Torture, recently
established and already quite widespread; the SOS Telephone
Friends, that brings many Christians from the various
Churches together to respond by telephone to the lonely people in the great cities and to all the men and women in distress
who need the comforting presence of a friendly and fraternal
voice; exchanges of observers at all levels of Church life (assemblies of bishops, Protestant or Anglican synods, Orthodox
conferences, local pastoral councils, priests' councils). I may
mention also gatherings of religious women from various
Churches; meetings of priests and Protestant pastors; various
mixed commissions and committees, official or private, at the
world, national and local levels; the regular meetings of
Church authorities; common schools of faith; ecumenical insti-
tutes; pastoral collaboration in various spheres at the parish
level; ecumenical twinnings of parishes, dioceses, or cathe-
drals; ecumenical groups for prayer, study of doctrine or the
Bible, or common action (helping migrants and the margina-
lized; fighting against alcoholism and unemployment; visiting
the prisons); groups of families in mixed marriages ("a real
bond of union between the Churches," as Father Beaupère has
called them), in which, together with priests and pastors, cou-
ples deepen their faith life and their conjugal life, reflect on
the Christian education of their children, and even go so far as
to set up what can properly be called a joint catechetical program.

This kind of pastoral work with mixed marriages is a re-markable advance and has led, at the instigation of the families themselves, to ecumenical celebrations of infant baptisms. It continues to be understood, of course, that there can be no baptism and thus no incorporation into Christ without an incorporation into a visible ecclesial community; for this reason it is a minister of a concrete confessional Church who performs the sacramental act in the name of that Church, and emphatically so, in order that the unicity of Christian baptism may find concrete expression through the participation in the celebration of the minister from the other Church, through the acceptance of spiritual responsibility for the child by both communities, and even by the recording of the baptism on the rolls of the Church which did not celebrate the sacrament.[34]

Mixed marriages are becoming more and more numerous. In France, for example, eighty percent on the average of the marriages with which Protestant pastors deal are mixed. They are no longer regarded as dangerous exceptions that are al-lowed with regret. Catholic discipline has followed the direc-tives of Vatican II: a dispensation from canonical form may be given for a serious reason, and the old "cautions" have now given way to a declaration of intention that is much more nu-anced and is drawn up by the concerned parties themselves. The celebration remains the primary responsibility of one of the ministers but the other may be involved in the prayer or the preaching. The celebration also now comes most often af-ter a course of pastoral preparation in which the ministers of the Churches concerned are involved.

The movement of "charismatic renewal" is also playing an ecumenical role at the level of prayer in the Spirit. Finally, my quick review, which cannot, of course, be exhaustive, would be seriously deficient if I did not mention the role and international influence of the Community of the Brothers of Taizé, which exerts such an attraction on the young, provides spiritual formation for all those received there, engages in theological study, and promotes help for the poorest and most abandoned.

OBSTACLES AND QUESTIONS

I cannot pass over the paradox that our common works and discussions and undertakings confront us with questions which, humanly speaking, we are incapable of resolving. The paths we have so joyously cleared and on which the Holy Spirit is setting up his trail-marks, his provisional beacons, run too often against obstacles which we do not know how to surmount.

These obstacles arise out of the classical doctrinal disputes which I mentioned earlier in my first chapter. Among these is the dispute over ministries between the Catholic Church and the Reformation Church. There is indeed a growing agreement on the structural function of the ordained ministry in the Church, its apostolicity, and the gift of the Spirit which it represents for the Church. Nonetheless, as I pointed out earlier, the question of ministries is still the most important barrier on the road to unity. For, as Fr. Sesboüé has remarked, "it is not enough to develop common convictions on the subject. The convictions must also be translated into actions through ecclesial decisions and acts of reconciliation which can only be the fruit of a profound conversion of the body made up of all the Churches. It is undoubtedly difficult to cross this threshold of irreversible decision."

I also reported earlier on the advances which have reduced classical disputes to the level of the psychological and the theological and in this way sought to eliminate causes of separation. But these advances in theological dialogue as well as the reconciliations effected by common action are faced with a serious obstacle that takes several forms.

There are those who interpret all advances or reconciliations as an abdication, a loss of identity, an infidelity to those ancestors who fought for their faith to the point of suffering torture and death for it. This attitude can be found, for example, in some French Protestants; it can doubtless be detected in Catholics here and there throughout the world. Their minority situation, produced by past history, explains this reaction. There are others who see all these advances, especially in the doctrinal area, as dangerous compromises. In his opening address to the General Meeting of the Secretariat for Christian Unity at Rome in November 1981, Cardinal Willebrands made some remarks on this point:

> There are some exercises in ingenuity that must be avoided, such as, for example, identifying the objective content of the faith with its exposition, organization and perception, with this or that theology, with this or that type of piety, with this or that kind of religious sensibility. Such efforts are an attack on catholicity and therefore on unity. We must avoid the temptation of identifying the truth of the faith, on which agreement is indeed required, with the formulation or formulations it has been given in the course of history.

The cardinal is here putting in different words what I said earlier about the "economy" practiced by the Council of Constantinople.

New questions and new divisions are also occurring within the Churches or between the Churches. There are new mentalities forming and new ideas of what the "real" problems are—those, for example, of the young and the not so young who consider ecumenism to be outmoded and who believe that the only real problem is unbelief and that the disputes between the Churches have to do with outdated institutions and thus no longer deserve attention by comparison with the demands of proclaiming the Gospel in our own day. There are new mentalities among Christians who say that they are seeking not so much the unity of the Churches as to live in an effective way the communion that exists between themselves and other Christians who have had the same experiences. There are new sets of problems among Christians who, consciously or unconsciously, are looking for a union of Christians without a union of Churches.

There is another and more substantial problem in the majority sectors of the different Churches: too many believers, because of the lack of persons to serve as associates or partners or because no attention has been paid to them, have not yet heard the call of the Spirit to ecumenism; they have not grasped its urgency, its requirements, and the legitimate and necessary sacrifices which the call entails. Yet ecumenism must be a dimension of the entire existence and pastoral activity of the Church and of the entire life of Christians.

We are faced with many other problems as well: disenchantment, for example, at the slow pace of ecumenical progress, or withdrawal into confessional identity which seems all the more precious to the extent that the future of the faith becomes uncertain. "Many people regard the preservation of the status quo as the only valid expression of tradition and identity. Yet should we not look upon the general crisis of faith as a challenge issued by the Holy Spirit to a new obedience of mind and heart? Is it not our duty to move forward together and to interpret together the signs of the times?"

There are still other problems: the gap between "specialists" in dialogue and certain "authorities" who are absorbed in the management of everyday affairs or paralyzed by the fear of seeing, if not their own power, their community disintegrate still more; the future of unity and the kind of union; the intermediate stages and the degree of initiative to be left to the local Churches in the process of restoring visible unity; the gradual implementation of "conciliarity" and the effective establishment of organs of "conciliar fellowship," such as, for example, "Christian Councils" or "Councils of Churches"; the pastoral ministry to families in mixed marriages: their sacramental life, the baptism and education of their children, an ecumenical catechesis; ethical problems (contraception, abortion, etc.); the rights of persons and peoples: peace, work, unemployment, violence. The ethical problems are located within the larger problem of anthropology, that is, of the conception and situation of the human person as these change their meaning due to the environing culture.

K. Rahner and J. B. Metz recently explained to us that Thomas Aquinas effected a transition from the cosmocentrism of antiquity to a Christian anthropocentrism and that insofar as modern thought is anthropocentric it is so on the basis of a theological a priori that is in turn based on faith.[35] Meanwhile, P. Eyt, following P. Ricoeur, has shown that the "philosophy of suspicion" and certain systematizations in the human sciences are offering us a real anti-humanism and that "theology must become more conscious of its obligation to act as a voice in behalf of the person and must do this in the power which comes from the word of God."[36]

It is clear that if such a new awareness is to be as evangelical as possible, it can only be ecumenical. Christians accept a common confession of faith regarding the human person and they must proclaim it. The Churches and individual Christians cannot speak or behave as if the various problems I have been listing did not exist. They must face up to them and reflect together on them. An ecumenism in the area of questions calls for an ecumenism in the area of answers. This ecumenism of common questions and common answers is the ecumenism of the Holy Spirit who, as Vatican II has shown, casts all of us into a crucible in which he alone can forge a new unity.

A final serious question, and one acutely felt, is the so-called question of intercommunion. The question involves the relationship between sacraments and faith, sacraments and Church, sacraments and unity.

First, a definition of terms. Intercommunion (an inexact term from the theological standpoint) is the permission given by a Church to its members for sharing eucharistic communion in another Church. The word also refers to the practice of Christians who take Communion at any and all eucharistic tables without concern for permission from the authorities of their Churches. Intercommunion, however, raises ecclesiological and disciplinary problems on which the Churches have taken carefully defined positions, as we shall see. The individual needs to inform himself or herself on these positions for the sake of an objectivity enlightened conscience.

In the Catholic Church the new *communicatio in sacris* (participation in sacred rites or objects) is given to the active participation in the Church's liturgy or sacraments that is granted in certain exceptional cases to Christians of another confession. "Eucharistic hospitality" means the admission to a Church's eucharistic table of Christians belonging to another Church that is not in full communion with the first.

The Orthodox and Catholic traditions have always maintained the principle of no *communicatio in sacris* with Christians not belonging to the same Church. The Protestant position is quite different: it would like to see sacramental and especially eucharistic hospitality practiced in a general and reciprocal way among all those who are united by one and the same baptism. These divergent positions are grounded in very different conceptions of the mystery of the visible Church. On the other hand, the very dynamism of reconciliation that is at work causes the remaining signs of division to be felt as very painful. A situation of tension is thus set up in the sphere of the sacraments. It is clear that this situation is becoming increasingly difficult for Christians, including Catholics, who have the ecumenical spirit but little theological formation, to live with and understand. It is a source of tensions, especially in mixed marriages and in groups most heavily involved in ecumenism.

If we are to gain a correct idea of the question of "intercommunion" or eucharistic hospitality, it is not enough to define the still quite different positions of the Churches. Also to be taken into account is the spiritual quality of the desire which many Christians keenly feel and strongly express for the sign of eucharistic communion with those outside the boundaries of their own Church. I am referring to Christians in mixed marriages and in ecumenical groups. Let me add that eucharistic communion should not be the occasion for precipitate sharing that minimizes divergences and shows a satisfaction with equivocal positions in the area of belief in the Eucharist. Eucharistic hospitality is not a universal solution to be adopted on the road to unity. The refusal to ask for eucharistic hospitality is also a way of walking in greater poverty and in deprivation, on the ecumenical road which is still, for Churches and individual Christians, a road of poverty, renunciation and obedience after the pattern of Christ.

In short, if we are to make progress in this painful question, we must develop still further the relation between Church and Eucharist at the ecclesiological level. We must also keep in mind the question of the mutual acceptance of ministries which is always present in the background because of its close connection with the sacramental structure of the Church and with the full reality of the Eucharist.

In face of this wall of still existing difficulties at the level of facts and of theological or non-theological factors, our prayer for unity daily becomes increasingly a prayer of petition and intercession, of metanoia, of personal and community self-emptying. We become penitents on account of that which we have "not yet received." The Holy Spirit is leading us into a fuller acceptance of the conversions required; if and as we respond, then, whatever the remaining obstacles, we will advance further in the directions of the rediscoveries and new forms of communion that he is bringing about.

REQUIREMENTS

Vatican II has reminded us that "there can be no ecumenism worthy of the name without interior conversion."[37]

This interior conversion has several aspects which it has been given us to experience in our ecumenical life.

It is a conversion of the heart, which through fraternal love teaches us to rediscover in common prayer and common action our very being and nature as Christians.

It is a conversion of the mind through the dialectic between the love of truth and the truth of love.

It is a conversion of mentalities leading us to the symbiosis or life together that is already a stage of partial but real communion, and ultimately to full and definitive communion.

Vatican II has also told us once again that "every renewal of the Church essentially consists in an increase of fidelity to its own calling. Undoubtedly this explains the dynamism of the movement toward unity."[38] The words are also a call to a confessional conversion on the part of all the Churches or Ecclesial Communities and, first and foremost, on the part of the Catholic Church to which the conciliar Decree is addressed. This conversion involves a dying to what is sinful in a confessional identity and a passing over into a life of visibly reconstituted ecclesial unity.

This kind of conversion is incumbent on all the members of the Churches, including those in authority, who must learn to differentiate between impossible sacrifices (indefectible fidelity to the truth of the Gospel), useless sacrifices (differences compatible with unity), and necessary sacrifices (our own share in the sin of division).

This ecclesial conversion must lead to decisions and acts of reconciliation that have to do with the faith, the life and the structure of the Church. What is needed is, in effect, to reorganize, in unity, the signs and realities proper to the mystery of the Church.

CONCLUSION:
THE GREAT WORKS OF GOD

On our twentieth century road to unity considerable advances have already been made, but many of them have not yet produced effects that can be discerned at present; this is because of the still remaining problems of which I have spoken. The Fathers of the Church emphasized the part played by maturation, ripening, delay and the passage of time in the divine pedagogy. St. Irenaeus went so far as to say that the Spirit had to get used to being with men.[1] John Paul II has repeatedly said that disputes which have gone on for centuries cannot be eliminated in a few years. On the other hand, if we consider the development of ecumenism, we must recognize that in our twentieth century the Holy Spirit has effected an astonishing acceleration of progress. The advance has been by small steps but also by giant steps.

Today, more than twenty years after the Council, the generations of Christians now living, but especially the young, are conscious primarily of what unites them rather than of what divides them. We are obsessed with the cry of Cardinal Bessarion (1395–1472): "What excuse can we give to justify our refusal to reunite? What will we say to God to justify this division of brothers and sisters, after Christ came down from heaven, took flesh and was crucified in order to unite us and make us a single flock? How will we excuse ourselves to future generations? More than that, how can we excuse ourselves to our contemporaries?"[2]

As we travel the road to unity we are in the position of Abraham as he is described in the Letter to the Hebrews: "By faith Abraham obeyed when he was called to go out to a place which he was to receive as an inheritance; and he went out, not knowing where he was to go. By faith he sojourned in the land of promise, as in a foreign land, living in tents with Isaac and Jacob. . . . For he looked forward to the city which has foundations, whose builder and maker is God" (Heb 11:8–11). This text applies admirably to the ecumenical journey, inasmuch as it singles out the exemplary faith that puts its hope in a person rather than claims to know something. On this journey, which has already taken us somewhat into the promised land of the restoration of full communion, the Spirit has been setting up provisional beacons that are intended to be removed one after the other and replaced by new, better and more profoundly meaningful ones, provided we are willing to advance step by step in fidelity to the light given to us; provided too, that we renounce the habit of measuring everything by the standard of dogmas or practices that have been part of a tradition; provided, finally, that we remain, not turned toward the past like Lot's wife (Lk 17:32), but open to the uncertain but radiant presence of the future like Mary. This is the Mary exalted by Martin Luther, who said: "She sang [the Magnificat] not for herself alone but for us all, to sing it after her. Now, these great works of God will neither terrify nor comfort anyone unless he believes that God has not only the power and the knowledge but also the willingness and hearty desire to do such great things."[3]

DATES AND REFERENCE POINTS

325	Ecumenical Council of Nicaea: Jesus the Christ is consubstantial with the Father.
381	Ecumenical Council of Constantinople: The Holy Spirit is God.
431	Ecumenical Council of Ephesus: Mary is Mother of God (Theotokos).
451	Ecumenical Council of Chalcedon: Unity of Christ's divinity and humanity in his one person.
1054	Reciprocal excommunications of the Churches of Rome and Constantinople.
1274	General Synod of the Western Church at Lyons: Abortive attempt at union with the Byzantine Churches.
1520	Luther excommunicated.
1530	The Augsburg Confession.
1531	The Church of England splits off from Rome.
1545–63	General Synod of the Western Church at Trent. Assertion of the Catholic Faith against Protestantism.
1869–70	General Synod of the Western Church at the Vatican: The Constitution *Pater Aeternus* on papal primacy.
1890	Conversations of Lord Halifax and Fr. Portal in Madeira.
1910	World conference of Protestant mission societies (in pagan lands) at Edinburgh.

1948	First, and constituent, General Assembly of the World Council of Churches, at Amsterdam
1962–65	General Synod of the Western Church at the Vatican.
1964	Paul VI promulgates the *Decree on Ecumenism.* (Nov. 21)
1966	The Secretariat for Christian Unity (Rome) becomes a department of the Roman Curia.

REDISCOVERIES:
IMPORTANT DATES
(TWENTIETH CENTURY)

	Catholic Church	Orthodox Church	Anglican Church	Protestant Churches
1910				Edinburgh: World Missionary Conference
1920		Encyclical Letter of the Church of Constantinople to all the Churches of the world	Lambeth Appeal	Creation of the International Missionary Council
1925				Stockholm: First world ecumenical conference Establishment of Life and Work
1927				Lausanne: First ecumenical conference on Faith and Order
1935	Fr. Couturier: Octave of Prayer for Unity			
1938		Utrecht: Merging of Life and Work with Faith and Order, with a view to forming the World Council of Churches.		
1948		Establishment of the World Council of Churches		
1952	International Catholic Conference on Ecumenical Questions			
1954		Evanston: Second General Assembly of the World Council of Churches		

1959	John XXIII announces the Second Vatican Council
1960	Creation of the Secretariat for Christian Unity
1961	Sending of observers to the General Assembly of the World Council of Churches — New Delhi: Third General Assembly of the World Council of Churches
1962	Observers invited to the Council—Opening of the Council — The World Council of Churches sends observers to the Council
1964	Meeting of Paul VI and Athenagoras in Jerusalem — Conciliar *Decree on Ecumenism* — Beginning of a dialogue of Catholics and the Lutheran World Federation
1965	Reciprocal lifting of excommunications — Creation of a Joint Working Group of the Roman Catholic Church and the World Council of Churches — Celebration of the word at Saint Paul Outside the Walls: Pope, Observers at the Council, and Council Fathers — Beginning of a dialogue between the Catholic Church and the World Methodist Council

	Catholic Church	Orthodox Church	Anglican Church	Protestant Churches
1966			Dr. Ramsey officially received at the Vatican	
1967	Exchange of visits by Paul VI and Athenagoras		Mixed Anglican-Roman Catholic commission	Contacts between the Catholic Church and the Bible Society
1971	Meeting of Paul VI and the Syrian Patriarch			
1973	Meeting of Paul VI and the Coptic Patriarch			
1979	John Paul II and Patriarch Dimitrios I establish the mixed Catholic-Orthodox Commission for theological dialogue			
1982			Final Report of ARCIC Visit of John Paul II to Canterbury	
1983	Document of Faith and Order (Lima) on Baptism, Eucharist and Ministry			
	Holy Year			Luther Year
	6th General Assembly of the World Council of Churches at Vancouver			

GLOSSARY[1]

Anathema (in classical Greek; something set up or devoted/accursed): A penalty which separates the person from the society of other Christians.

Autocephalous (Churches) (from Greek: *autos* = self, and *kephale* = head): A self-governing Church, which is recognized as capable

    (1) of electing its own primate (patriarch or archbishop);

    (2) of consecrating the holy chrism needed for the sacrament of confirmation. All the autocephalous Churches together make up the universal Orthodox Church. Until 1848 (encyclical letter of the patriarchs in response to Pope Pius IX), questions of general discipline were resolved by agreement of the four patriarchs (the pentarchy minus Rome); since 1961 the pentarchy has been replaced by panorthodox assemblies: twenty-one delegates, one from each autocephalous Church, including the archbishops of the United States and Japan.

Azymous (in Greek: without yeast):

    (a) unleavened bread used for the Jewish Passover;

    (b) unleavened bread used in the Latin Church for the Eucharist;

    (c) in 1 Cor 5:7 azymous refers to the absence of corruption or, in positive terms, integrity.

Baptists: Communities who admit to baptism only adults who have already had experience of the Christian life. The Baptists separated from the Church of England in the seventeenth century. The Baptist Churches, which are congregationalist in polity, constitute a worldwide important branch of Protestantism.

Cappadocians (Cappadocian Fathers): A group of outstanding bishops, all from Cappadocia, in the fourth century: Basil of Caesarea; Gregory of Nyssa, Basil's brother; Gregory Nazianzus; and Amphilochius of Iconium, who is less well known. The Cappadocian Fathers are also called the neo-Nicaeans, because around 370 they offered a creative explanation, in the language of their period and culture, of the teaching of the first Ecumenical Council of Nicaea (321), in which they defined more closely the relationships between the one divine essence and the three persons of the Holy Trinity.

Christology: In theology, the study of the person and mission of Christ.

Circumincession (the Greek term *perichoresis* is used in Eastern theology):

(a) the continuous interchange of life among the three divine persons;

(b) the Fathers of the Church also applied the term circumincession to the reciprocal exchange of life between the Word of God and the humanity of Jesus to which the Word has united himself through the incarnation.

The union of the two natures in the one person of the Word establishes what the theologians call the "communication of idioms," i.e., of the properties of each of the two natures.

Ecclesiology: The part of Christian doctrine that deals with the Church; differences in ecclesiology are at the heart of the ecumenical dialogue. A "communionist ecclesiology" is one that moves beyond a juridical ecclesiology which is based on the notion of society, and emphasizes communion in the Holy Spirit.

Economy:

(a) In the Greek Fathers and still in Orthodox theology, the part of theology devoted to the history of salvation and in particular to the incarnation of the Son (the other part of theology being the study of the mystery of God in himself and of God as creator and preserver of all things). The Latin Fathers translated the Greek *oikonomia* as *dispositio.*

(b) Again in the Eastern Church, the doctrine according to which, because of circumstances and for the sake of a greater interior good, the Church tolerates, and does not penalize in the ways provided, actions not in conformity with the ecclesiastical regulations now in force. Economy, in this sense, is contrasted with *akribeia,* "exactness," that is, the strict application of ecclesiastical law.

(c) The same principle of "economy" is applied in certain cases by the Roman Church, for example, in the case of a *sanatio in radice* (a "healing at the root") of a marriage.

(d) "Economy" in sense *b* is based on a sense of the transcendence of the divine mystery and therefore of the inadequacy of all the human forms that are used to express it. Economy seems to be the natural consequence of apophatic theology in the area of the exercise of ecclesiastical authority. Though it may be argued that Western thought has potential equivalents for the terms and attitudes involved, "economy" in the Eastern sense has nonetheless a nuance that eludes these identifications, however accurate.

This nuance is due to the two different approaches of East and West to the divine mystery, and to the two ways of responding to the gift of God. It would perhaps be more accurate to speak of two different dominants that prevail through a range of divergent styles and manners.

The union of Churches, which also, and inevitably, has its juridicial aspects, might well apply this principle of economy in certain cases.

Ecumenism: The movement raised up by the Holy Spirit for

the restoration of unity among all Christians, in order that the world may believe in Jesus Christ. The participants in this movement are those who invoke the Triune God and confess Jesus Christ as Savior and Lord and who, while remaining within the communities in which they have heard the Gospel, aspire to form the one Church of God, single and visible, truly universal, sent to the entire world in order that the world may be converted to the Gospel and be saved for the glory of God.

Epiclesis (Greek: invocation): In the eucharistic liturgy, the invocation of the Holy Spirit on the assembly and on the bread and wine.

Eschatology (from Greek: *ta eschata* = the final things): The study of all that has to do with the fulfillment at the end of time of the universal redemptive work of Christ. This fulfillment is already present in germinal form in Christian life but is not yet fully developed; this completion requires the parousia, that is, the final coming of Christ and the glorious inauguration of his Kingdom through the resurrection of the dead and the final or general judgment.

—The name eschatology is also applied to everything in Christian life that is in conformity with the promise of that fulfillment.

—The rediscovery of the "eschatological dimension" of the Church as a people en route to the coming Kingdom can help to overcome certain historical oppositions within the ecumenical dialogue.

Ethics (Greek: *ethike* = morality): The study of the norms for human conduct. In the area of ecumenism, ethics raises the question of the common responsibility of Christians in a world that is searching for the value and meaning of life, rather than for rules to govern what is allowed or forbidden.

—The present differences among Christians at the level of "law" (for example, the positions taken on abortion) could well be changed through ecumenical dialogue into a common quest for the purposes of a common witness.

Metanoia (from Greek; = repentance):

(a) in the broadest sense, the return to God of the sinner who hears the call to repentance;

(b) in a narrower sense, the discovery of Christ, which leads the person to baptism and into the new life of the spirit (Acts 2:38);

(c) the term metanoia is also applied to the Church to mean that all the Christian communities involved in the ecumenical movement should be open to the changes of perspective, mentality, heart and behavior which the Spirit asks of us for the sake of reconciliation.

Orthodox (from Greek: *orthos* = right, true; and *doxa* = opinion):

(a) One who professes a "right *or* correct faith." In this sense Catholics are "orthodox," just as the Orthodox rightly claim to be "catholic." In the High Middle Ages the terms "catholic" and "orthodox" were used interchangeably.

(b) Historically, the word orthodox was applied to the Church which remained faithful to the faith as defined at the Council of Chalcedon (451). In this sense, both Catholics and Byzantines are orthodox.

(c) After the iconoclastic persecution of 842 and after the separation of 1054 the Byzantine Churches described themselves as "Orthodox."

(d) In the Arab Near East the ancient Eastern non-Chalcedonian Churches are also called "Orthodox." Thus we speak of the Coptic Orthodox and the Syrian Orthodox, even though they are not part of the Church that is in union with Constantinople, i.e., the "Melkite" Church.

SHORT BIBLIOGRAPHY

Beauvery, Robert, Bertrand Rollin, Louis-Marie Chauvet, and Jacques-Elisée Desseaux. *L'Eucharistie: De Jésus aux chrétiens d'aujourd'hui.* Paris: Droguet et Ardant.

Bosc, Jean. *La foi chrétienne.* Paris: Presses Universitaires de France.

Deltheil, Frank, Roger Mehl, Georges Richard-Molard, and Daniel Robert. *Le Protestantisme, hier, demain.* Paris: Buchet-Chastel.

Desseaux, Jacques-Elisée. *Dialogues théologiques et accords oecuméniques.* Paris: Cerf, 1982.

Evdokimov, Paul. *L'Orthodoxie.* Paris: Desclée De Brouwer.

Neill, Stephen. *Anglicanism.* Baltimore: Penguin, 1965[3].

Tillard, J.M.R., O.P. *The Bishop of Rome,* tr. by John de Satge. Wilmington, Del.: Michael Glazier, 1981.

Villain, Maurice. *Unity: A History and Some Reflections,* tr. by J.R. Foster. Baltimore: Helicon, 1963.

NOTES

CHAPTER I.

1. Y. Congar, *After Nine Hundred Years. The Background of the Schism Between the Eastern and Western Churches* (New York, 1959), 3.

2. Paul VI, Letter *Lugduni* to Cardinal Willebrands on the 700th Anniversary of the Council of Lyon (October 5, 1974), in *L'Osservatore Romano,* October 20, 1974.

3. Cf. W. De Vries, *Orient et Occident. Les structures ecclésiales vues dans l'histoire des sept premiers conciles oecuméniques* (Paris, 1974).

4. Tr. in A. Flannery (ed.), *Vatican Council II. The Conciliar and Postconciliar Documents* (Collegeville, 1975), 466.

5. K. Adam, *One and Holy,* tr. by C. Hastings (New York, 1951), 6.

6. Cited in L. Pastor, *The History of the Popes* 9, tr. by R.F. Kerr (2nd ed.; St. Louis, 1923), 134–35.

7. R. Aubert, in *Nouvelle Histoire de l'Eglise* 1 (Paris, 1963), 16.

8. From the hymn *Our God He Is a Castle Strong,* tr. in U.S. Leupold (ed.), *Liturgy and Hymns* (Luther's Works 53; Philadelphia, 1965), 285.

9. Y. Congar, *Vraie et fausse réforme dans l'Eglise* (Unam Sanctam 72; Paris, 1969), 325 and 478.

10. In *L'Avenir* (Semaine des intellectuels catholiques, 1963; Paris, 1964), 228.

Chapter II.

1. A. Camus, "The Unbeliever and Christians," in his *Resistance, Rebellion and Death,* tr. by J. O'Brien (New York, 1960), 52–53.

2. T.F. Stransky and J.B. Sheerin (eds.), *Doing the Truth in Charity: Statements of Pope Paul VI, Popes John Paul I, John Paul II, and the Secretariat for Promoting Christian Unity, 1964–1980* (Ecumenical Documents I; New York, 1982), 238.

3. Stransky-Sheerin, 246–48.

4. Patriarch Maximos IV Sayegh, "The Eastern Role in Christian Reunion," in Maximos IV Sayegh (ed.), *The Eastern Churches and Catholic Unity* (New York, 1963), 61 and 56.

5. Common Declaration of Paul VI and Athenagoras of Constantinople at the close of their second meeting, Jerusalem, January 6, 1964, in *The Pope Speaks* 9 (1963–64) 283.

6. Homily of John Paul II in Holy Spirit Church, Istanbul, November 29, 1979, in Stransky-Sheerin, 208.

7. G. Tavard, *Petite histoire du Mouvement oecuménique* (Paris, 1960).

8. Cited in R.C. Morse, *History of the North American Young Men's Christian Associations* (New York, 1963), 279.

9. *Lambeth Conferences (1867–1930)* (London, 1948), 297.

10. M. Boegner, *The Long Road to Unity: Memories and Anticipations,* tr. by R. Hague (London, 1970), 32.

11. This passage is from Mott's closing address as reported in *World Missionary Conference, 1910* 10. *The History and Records of the Conference* (New York, n.d.), 346, 348.

12. Text in C.H. Patelos (ed.), *The Orthodox Church in the Ecumenical Movement. Doctrinal Statements, 1902–1975* (Geneva, 1978), 40–43.

13. Boegner, *op. cit.,* 37.

14. Edinburgh Report, no. 189, in L. Vischer (ed.), *A Documentary History of the Faith and Order Movement, 1927–1963* (St. Louis, 1963), 42.

15. *The First Assembly of the World Council of Churches,*

Amsterdam. August 22–September 4, 1948, ed. by W.A. Visser 't Hooft (New York, 1949), 197.

16. *The New Delhi Report: The Third Assembly of the World Council of Churches, 1961,* ed. by W.A. Visser 't Hooft (New York, 1962), 426.

17. *The Pope Speaks* 9 (1963–64) 283.

18. Stransky-Sheerin, 278.

19. *Ecumenical Review* 34 (1982) 295.

CHAPTER III.

1. *Common Witness.* Study Document of the Joint Working Group of the Roman Catholic Church and the World Council of Churches (Geneva, 1980), 12.

2. *Decree on Ecumenism* 12, tr. in A. Flannery (ed.), *Vatican Council II: The Conciliar and Postconciliar Documents* (Collegeville, 1975), 462.

3. Introduction and text of the message in *Unité des Chrétiens,* July 1979, 6ff.

4. "La théologie depuis 1939," in his *Situation et tâches présentes de la théologie* (Paris, 1967), 38.

5. J.E. Desseaux, *Dialogues théologiques et accords oecuméniques* (Paris, 1982).

6. Cf. J.M. Tillard, "Vers une profession de foi commune," *Documentation catholique,* no. 1752 (November 19, 1978).

7. *Decree on Ecumenism* 11 (Flannery, 462).

8. *Documentation catholique,* no. 1450 (June 20, 1965) 1116.

9. Published by the Secretariat for Christian Unity, April 16, 1970; text in Stransky-Sheerin, 59–74 at 65.

10. Published by the Secretariat for Christian Unity, August 15, 1970; text in Stransky-Sheerin, 75–88 at 81.

11. Published by the Sacred Congregation for the Doctrine of the Faith, June 24, 1973; text in *The Pope Speaks* 18 (1975) 145–57 at 150–53.

12. J. de Baciocchi, "Accord des Dombes et théologie oe-cuménique" *Istina* 19 (1974) 163ff.

13. *Documentation catholique,* no. 1752 (November 19, 1978).

14. Citing Gregory Nazianzus, *Or.* XXI.

15. St. Basil, *De fide* I.

16. Severus of Antioch, *Liber contra impium grammati-cum* III, 2 (Sources chrétiennes 93:94).

17. Address at the Patriarchal Cathedral of St. George, Is-tanbul, July 25, 1967 (Stransky-Sheerin, 182).

18. Cited in G. Martelet, *Oser croire en l'Eglise* (Paris, 1968), 68.

19. J. Ratzinger, "Pronostics sur l'avenir de l'oecumén-isme," *Proche-Orient chrétien* 26 (1976) 215.

20. Cf. n. 5, above.

21. *Confessions in Dialogue: A Survey of Bilateral Con-versations among World Confessional Families,* 1962–1971 (Geneva, 1972).

22. "A Workbook of Bibliographies for the Study of Inter-church Dialogues," *The Bulletin of the Centro pro Unione* (Rome), nos. 15, 17 and 19.

23. On this subject see the remarkable book of J.M. Til-lard, *The Bishop of Rome,* tr. by John de Satge (Wilmington, Del., 1983).

24. ARCIC, *The Final Report (Windsor, September, 1981)* (Washington, D.C., 1982).

25. Ratzinger, *art. cit.,* 214.

26. Paul VI and Mar Ignatius Jacob III (Stransky-Sheering, 238).

27. J.A. Moehler, *L'unité dans l'eglise, ou le principe du catholicisme d'après l'esprit des Pères des trois premiers siècles* (Unam Sanctam 2; Paris, 1938), 125, 145–46.

28. In his address to the Secretariat for Christian Unity, April 28, 1967.

29. Cyprian, *De oratione dominica* 23, cited in *Lumen gentium* 4 (Flannery, 352).

30. *Faith and Order Louvain 1971: Study Reports and*

Documents (Faith and Order Paper No. 59; Geneva: World Council of Churches, 1971) 225–229.

31. *Breaking Barriers: Nairobi 1975,* ed. by D.M. Paton (Grand Rapids, 1976), 60; the report is citing the Salamanca conference.

32. *Unité des chrétiens,* no. 27 (July 1977) 19.

33. *Breaking Barriers: Nairobi 1975,* 317–18.

34. See "La célébration oecuménique des baptêmes d'enfants," a Note of the Catholic-Protestant Commission of France, in *Documentation catholique,* no. 1673 (April 6, 1975), 318–20.

35. J.B. Metz, *Christliche Anthropozentrik* (Munich, 1962). French tr.: *L'Homme. L'anthropocentrique chrétien: Pour une interprétation de la philosophie de saint Thomas* (Paris, 1968).

36. P. Eyt, "La théologie et la mort de l'homme," *Nouvelle revue théologique* 96 (1974) 478.

37. *Decree on Ecumenism* 7 (Flannery, 460).

38. *Decree on Ecumenism* 6 (Flannery, 459).

CONCLUSION

1. *Adversus haereses* III, 20, 3.

2. Dogmatic Discourse to the Greeks, April 15, 1439.

3. Luther, *The Magnificat,* tr. by A.T.W. Steinhauser, in *Luther's Works* 21 (St. Louis, 1956), 306.

GLOSSARY

1. Cf. J.E. Desseaux, *Nouveau vocabulaire oecuménique* (Paris, 1980), which contains 602 words, of which 133 are the names of persons.